embraced *by* holiness

Other New Hope books
by Kathy Howard

Before His Throne: Discovering the Wonder of Intimacy with a Holy God

Fed Up with Flat Faith: 10 Attitudes and Actions to Pump Up Your Faith

Unshakeable Faith: 8 Traits for Rock-Solid Living

God's Truth Revealed: Biblical Foundations for the Christian Faith

kathy howard

embraced *by* holiness

the path to God's daily presence

NEW HOPE
PUBLISHERS
Gospel-Centered. Missions-Driven.

BIRMINGHAM, ALABAMA

New Hope® Publishers
PO Box 12065
Birmingham, AL 35202-2065
NewHopeDigital.com
New Hope Publishers is a division of WMU®.

Library of Congress Control Number: 2013955345

Unless otherwise noted, Scripture quotations are taken from THE HOLY BIBLE, NEW INTERNATIONAL VERSION®, NIV® Copyright © 1973, 1978, 1984, 2011 by Biblica, Inc.® Used by permission. All rights reserved worldwide.

Scripture quotations marked NLT are taken from the Holy Bible, New Living Translation, copyright © 1996, 2004, 2007 by Tyndale House Foundation. Used by permission of Tyndale House Publishers, Inc., Carol Stream, Illinois 60188. All rights reserved.

Scripture quotations marked AMP are taken from the Amplified® Bible, Copyright © 1954, 1958, 1962, 1964, 1965, 1987 by The Lockman Foundation. Used by permission.

Cover and Interior Design: Glynese Northam

ISBN-10: 1-59669-409-2
ISBN-13: 978-1-59669-409-5

N144115 • 0614 • 3M1

dedication

To my oldest baby, Kelley. It's such a joy to watch you pursue holiness out of love for your Savior. Keep working it out! Philippians 2:12.

contents

acknowledgments

God has blessed my life with an abundance of godly women. Several of them have allowed me to share glimpses of their faith walk in this book: Denise, Lisa, Janet, Stephanie, Linda, Jenny, and Stacy. Thank you for your friendship and your example.

I am honored to work with New Hope Publishers. Andrea Mullins, Joyce Dinkins, Maegan Roper, and the rest of the staff work tirelessly to further the kingdom. Thank you for your ministry!

Much gratitude and big hugs to the women's ministry team and my Bible study friends at The Woodlands First Baptist Church. Thank you, ladies, for all your prayers, words of encouragement, and support. I love you all!

introduction

Would you like to sit next to God and snuggle up against His side? To be so close you could hear Him breathe? There would be no distance between the two of you, no barriers to prevent you from drawing near. You could linger in His presence and rest in the circle of His embrace.

All of us desire to experience this kind of intimate relationship with our heavenly Father. Yet, we often feel disconnected. We may even sense that something blocks our path to deep, personal companionship with God.

According to Scripture, a life of holiness can pave the way for greater intimacy in our relationship with God. King David, described as a man after God's own heart (Acts 13:22), understood the connection between a holy life and experiencing God's presence.

> *Who may worship in your sanctuary, LORD? Who may enter your presence on your holy hill? Those who lead blameless lives and do what is right, speaking the truth from sincere hearts.*
>
> (PSALM 15:1–2 NLT)

Unholy living floods believers' lives with the natural consequences of sin, including distance and strain in our relationships with our holy God. But a journey toward holiness is also a journey toward intimacy with God. As we embrace the holy life God calls us to, we are embraced by the Holy One Himself.

During the six weeks of this study, we will search God's Word to answer questions such as these:

- Why do I need to be holy?

- What is holiness?

- What does a holy life look like?

- Is holiness worth it?

- Is holiness really possible and how?

My prayer for us—you and me—as we go through this study of God's Word, is that He will give us a deeper understanding of His holiness and overwhelm us with a desire to share in it. As we seek holiness, may we experience the fullness of God's presence and be embraced by holy.

arms open wide

Our neighbors are building a fence. They moved in several months ago, but until recently the property line between our driveway and their backyard was wide open. With no barrier between our properties, I noticed when the dad played catch with his three sons, and I was able to enjoy the beautiful landscaping around their patio.

But all that began to change when I left town last week. The first things I noticed when I got home were the sturdy wooden posts firmly planted in the ground every few feet between our yards. Within days, cedar fencing replaced my unobstructed view of my neighbors and their yard.

I'm not against suburban fences. This one will benefit them and us. But watching that physical fence go up reminded me of other kind of fences we tend to build, particularly between ourselves and God. Our heavenly Father longs for intimate fellowship with us. He invites us to know Him fully and deeply. Yet the lack of holiness in our lives serves as a barrier.

Holy defines God's divine nature. In His holiness, He remains separate from everything sinful. Therefore, to experience deep intimacy with God, we must share in His holiness. God longs to draw us close, so He calls us to live holy lives. Sin builds barriers and creates distance between each of us and God. Holiness breaks down walls and fosters fellowship.

In our first week of study, we will explore God's holiness and discover why holiness matters in our lives. We will also hear God's call to holiness, His invitation to fellowship with Him. With arms wide open, He beckons you to draw near, to close the distance between you and Him. Can you hear Him call your name?

13

just like our Father

To help mark the occasion of my parents' 50th wedding anniversary, my brother put together a slide show of photos taken over the years. The evening before the big party, our family sat together looking through the images. A photo taken of my mom and dad in the late 1970s popped up on the screen. I had to look twice to confirm that it was Mom and not me staring back at me in the image. "Well, I guess you know what you'll look like in about 30 years," my brother remarked. *Yeah*, I thought. *Just like Mom looks now!*

Physically, I highly resemble my mother. I inherited her green eyes and angular facial features. Our voices sound like stereo. When people look at me, they immediately know I'm related to Margaret. Similarly, I should resemble my heavenly Father enough that people will know I'm His child. When people spend time with me, I should remind them of God. When Christians live holy lives, we reflect God's character to the world.

Would you use the word *holy* to describe yourself? If you said no, you have a lot of company. According to a poll by the Barna Group, only 29 percent of Americans who claim to have a personal, saving relationship with Jesus Christ (referred to as *born again* by Barna) consider themselves to be holy.

Do you think God wants you to be holy? Forty-six percent of born-again Americans say yes. That means the majority—about 54 percent—either don't think God wants them to be holy or they just don't know. Let's see what the Bible says.

Read the following Scripture passages and record what they teach about holiness. Include God's expectations for our holiness and why we should be holy.

Leviticus 20:7–8

Romans 12:1

Ephesians 1:3–4

Even this small sampling of Scripture should leave no room for doubt in our minds: God commands His people to be holy. Holiness is not a suggestion or a lifestyle reserved for the superspiritual. It is a command, an act of obedience for all believers.

To reinforce God's command for holiness, read 1 Thessalonians 4:1–8 and answer the following multiple-choice questions:

Paul instructed Christians in Thessalonica to live holy lives so they would:
a. Have to struggle to live rightly.
b. Be laughed at by their neighbors.
c. Please God.

Our lives will become holy:
a. Overnight.
b. Progressively over time as we continue to obey God.
c. Never, it's impossible.

Those who accept God's call to live a holy life:
a. Accept God Himself.
b. Obey God's will.
c. Acknowledge Jesus' authority in their life.
d. All of the above.

In his book, *The Pursuit of Holiness*, Jerry Bridges provides a helpful definition of *holiness*: "To be holy is to be morally blameless. It is to be separated from sin and, therefore, consecrated to God. The word signifies 'separation to God, and the conduct befitting those so separated.'" When I chase after holiness, I acknowledge that I belong to God. Because I am His, I should want to live a life that pleases Him and not the world.

Many Christians think a holy life is too difficult. They recognize the truth that God commands His children to be holy and want to please

Him, but life gets in the way. Others compare themselves to the Christians around them and think they're doing pretty good. But God doesn't call us to "pretty good." He calls us to holiness.

Keep in mind, whatever God requires of His children, He also supplies. God requires holiness, but His Spirit provides the power to turn away from sin. God calls us to holiness and God provides what we need to be holy.

But, why would we want to be holy? One reason is found in the very nature of holiness. (The basic meaning of *holy* is to be "set apart.") We are set apart *from* something and *to* something. As Christians we are set apart from the world—set free from its sinful ways and our own fleshly desires (Romans 12:1–2; 1 Peter 1:14). And we are set apart to God (Leviticus 20:26). We are unfettered from the bondage of sin and loosed to draw close to God. Thus, God's call to holiness is a call to freedom.

Nancy Leigh DeMoss elaborates on the freedom holiness brings in her book, *Holiness: The Heart God Purifies:*

> Why do we make holiness out to be some austere obligation or burden to be borne, when the fact is that to be holy is to be clean, to be free from the weight and the burden of sin? Why would we cling to our sin any more than a leper would refuse to part with his oozing sores, given the opportunity to be cleansed of his leprosy? To pursue holiness is to move toward joy—joy infinitely greater than any earthly delights can offer."

Scripture reveals many more blessings of a holy life. We will take a closer look at these in Week Five, but let's get a glimpse now.

Read the Scripture passages below and write the benefits of living a holy life.

Deuteronomy 7:6

Psalm 24:3–5

Hebrews 12:14

Are you ready to explore holiness? I am honored to be your guide on this journey. This freedom trek will take us from the base of God's holy mountain to the foot of Christ's Cross and beyond. Let's get started.

As we close today, write a prayer to God expressing your desire to understand His holiness and how He wants to work in your life.

getting to know Him

Our oldest daughter, Kelley, worked part-time all throughout university and still made excellent grades. During the last year of her undergraduate degree, I had the opportunity to meet her boss and several of her co-workers. They literally raved about her—her work ethic, her character, her personality. Her boss even gave me credit for a "wonderful job of raising such a terrific young woman."

Our parenting has not been the only influence in our daughter's life, but who she has become does reflect on me and her dad. She has made us look pretty good! However, there was an incident when she was about four that cast a pretty dim light on us as parents.

One Monday night we received a call from Kelley's Sunday School teacher. I could tell she was dreading the conversation. Kelley had used a four-letter word in class. "If it had been the first time," the teacher said she wouldn't have bothered us, but Kelley had shared the expletive several times with her young Sunday School chums. We weren't sure where she picked it up, but it certainly wasn't the way we wanted her to represent the Howard family.

If you are a Christian, you are God's child, His representative. The way you live is a reflection on the God to whom you belong. He calls us to correctly reflect His nature to the world.

Read 1 Peter 1:14–16. On what truth does God base His command to be holy?

Describe the behavior God contrasts with holiness?

Before we experienced God's great salvation, we "lived in ignorance," fulfilling our fleshly desires. But God has "given us new birth into a living hope" (1 Peter 1:3). Therefore, we can respond with obedience, joyfully anticipating our eternal inheritance. This new life of obedience is to be a holy life, based on the very nature of the God who saved us. As we saw in Day 1, our call to holiness is consistent throughout Scripture—both the Old and the New Testaments. In fact, the Apostle Peter quoted from Leviticus 11:44–45: "Be holy, because I am holy." God does not change (Malachi 3:6); His expectations for His children do not change.

We are to be holy because our God is holy. Since our holiness is to be a reflection of God's holiness, that's where we must begin our journey toward holiness. What does it mean that God is holy?

Read the Scripture passages listed below. List any facts and descriptive words and phrases you find in each one that help you understand God's holiness. (I've completed the first one as an example.)

Exodus 15:11
No one is like God; majestic; awesome; works wonders

Psalm 96:8–9

Proverbs 9:10

Isaiah 57:15

The Hebrew adjective translated as "holy" in Leviticus 11:44–45 and many other passages is *qadosh*. It describes that which is "distinct from the common or profane." In reference to God, it means His character is "totally good and entirely without evil." Not only is He "free from the moral imperfections and frailties common to man," He is "absolutely separate from evil." In one of his letters, the Apostle John painted a word picture that will help us understand this concept.

Read 1 John 1:5. On the line below, place an X to represent where God falls on the spectrum.
Light _____ Darkness

Throughout Scripture the words *light* and *darkness* are used metaphorically. *Light* represents godly characteristics such as righteousness, goodness, truth, life, justice, and salvation. *Darkness* stands for the antithesis of *light*, specifically evil and wickedness.

In your own words, write what it means that God is holy. (Consider the definition for holy and John's light/darkness metaphor when writing your description.)

God is the epitome of holiness. He is so separate from and above us in His holiness that we cannot even fully grasp its meaning. The word *majesty* is used to communicate this idea. Some refer to this as the "otherness" of God. However, our inability to completely understand God's holiness should not stop us from contemplating it.

Below are several quotes from respected theologians and Bible teachers describing the holiness of God. As you read them, underline words or phrases that deepen your understanding of God's holy nature.

> God's holiness is more than just separateness. His holiness is also transcendent. . . . To transcend is to rise above something, to go above and beyond a certain limit. . . . Transcendence describes His supreme and absolute greatness. . . . Transcendence describes God in His consuming majesty, His exalted loftiness.
> — R. C. SPROUL, *THE HOLINESS OF GOD*

Holy is the way God is. To be holy He does not conform to a standard. He is that standard. He is absolutely holy with an infinite, incomprehensible fullness of purity that is incapable of being other than it is. He is holy, His attributes are holy; that is, whatever we think of as belonging to God must be thought of as holy.

— A. W. TOZER, *THE KNOWLEDGE OF THE HOLY*

God's holiness then is perfect freedom from all evil....The absolute holiness of God should be of great comfort and assurance to us. If God is perfectly holy, then we can be confident that His actions toward us are always perfect and just. . . . Because He is holy, all His actions are holy.

— JERRY BRIDGES, *THE PURSUIT OF HOLINESS*

"Be holy, because I am holy." God is the plumb line or standard for our holiness. Humans are created in His image. God's original intent was for us to be holy like our Maker is holy. God's purpose has not changed. He still calls His people to holiness, to Christlikeness. God is both the reason we should be holy — and as we'll see in the weeks ahead — the reason we can be holy.

As we end today's study, spend a few moments contemplating the holiness of God. In the space below, write a prayer of praise to our holy God.

treasured by God

Before sin entered the world, the first man and woman experienced and enjoyed perfect, unhindered fellowship with their Creator. Just imagine — no fences, no walls, no barriers. Nothing stood in the way of sweet intimacy with God because their lives perfectly reflected His character — just as God designed (Genesis 2). "For he chose us in him before the creation of the world to be holy and blameless in his sight" (Ephesians 1:4).

Before God made the stars He called us to be holy. But Adam and Eve chose their own way of rebellion and sin separated humanity from God. But then, and now, God calls His children back to holiness. He urges us to come out of the bondage of sin and live in freedom. The freedom to draw close to Him again.

The nation of Israel provides a physical picture of this spiritual reality. After enduring slavery in Egypt for 400 years, Israel called out to God to deliver them from bondage.

Read Exodus 3:7–8 and fill in the blanks.

God saw their _____ . He heard them _____ and was concerned about their _____ . He came down to _____ them and to bring them into a _____ and _____ land.

Burdened with slavery, God's people looked to Him for salvation. In His mercy — and to display His power — God raised a deliverer, Moses, and then led His people into freedom. Three months after their exodus, God reminded Israel of His hand and His purposes.

 Read Exodus 19:1–6.

What did God do for the people of Israel?

What were His purposes for them?

What responsibilities did Israel have?

God brought Israel out of Egypt and made them His own. Even though the earth and everything in it belongs to God (Psalm 24:1), He declared the nation of Israel to be special — a holy nation and His "treasured possession" (Exodus 19:5). God made a covenant with Israel. God provided salvation, purpose, and life. Israel's obligation was obedience. God's treasured possession was to be a nation of priests, a light to the Gentiles, an intermediary between our holy God and an unholy world. This call required holiness.

Unfortunately, Israel failed to answer God's call and the consequences of their disobedience were great. Yet finally, after 40 years of wandering in the wilderness and the death of an entire generation, Israel stood on the edge of the Promised Land again. The Book of Deuteronomy records Moses' charge to the new generation. He recounts God's deliverance, call, and expectations. But how was Israel to live out this call to holiness in the Promised Land? They didn't have to wonder. God gave them specific instructions.

 Read Deuteronomy 7:1–6.

Summarize what God told the people to do when they entered the Promised Land.

Why were these drastic actions necessary? (See vv. 4 and 6.)

Scan Deuteronomy 7:12–16. What would be the results of Israel's obedience?

Israel had a big job ahead. God acknowledged the relatively small size of Israel compared to the nations they would encounter (v. 7). He knew this fact would cause anxiety. "You may say to yourselves, 'These nations are stronger than we are. How can we drive them out?'" (v. 17).

Read Deuteronomy 7:18–19. How did God reassure the Israelites?

Week 1
Day 3
24

A life of holiness can seem like a daunting task. We stand on the edge of the Promised Land with the blessings of God before us, yet we may lack the courage to move forward. What if obedience is too hard? What if God asks me to give up something I'm too weak to leave behind? What if the lure of the world is stronger than my resolve?

The way God worked in the life of His holy nation, Israel, parallels the way God still works today. He called Israel to live as a holy nation. This required purging the land of anything and everything that would draw their hearts away from God. They had to fight, but they were not responsible for the outcome (see vv. 1–2). As they moved forward in obedience, God would go before them in power, delivering the enemies into their hands.

Apply this biblical principle to your own life. As you obediently answer God's call to live a holy life, what will God do?

Write a prayer below expressing any fears and anxieties you have about responding to God's call to holiness.

day four

grateful hearts

We all have them—those funny family stories. The stories that, when retold, bring peals of laughter from everyone. Well, almost everyone. Sometimes one family member simply responds with an embarrassed chuckle. One of our funniest family memories involves our daughter, Sarah, and a turnstile.

It was the last week of summer and time to get ready for a new school year. Back then we lived in a small town about 25 miles outside Calgary, Alberta, Canada. The kind of shopping we needed to do required a trip to the city. So the three kids and I piled in the minivan and headed off for a day in Calgary.

We had almost hit the city limits when the smallest voice from the backseat announced he had gotten into the van without any shoes. Mom made a quick decision. We would not return home; six-year-old Mark needed new shoes anyway. Our first stop would be the sporting goods store not far into the city.

It didn't take long to pick out a nice pair of sneakers and socks and get to the checkout. While trying to explain to the checker why I was paying for an empty box, I heard a familiar scream close behind me. Sarah, our nine-year-old, had somehow managed to get herself caught in the turnstile at the store entrance.

I can't even explain how she did it because I didn't see it happen. The best I can determine is she tried to push through the turnstile on the wrong side where it spun under a crossbar. When she discovered she couldn't get through that way, she tried to back out, but instead wedged herself between the turning tripod and the stationary crossbar. Head and shoulders hung out one side, and her lower half hung out the other.

She wasn't hurt, but she was angry. While she continued to scream, the rest of us couldn't help but laugh—while trying to help her, of course. But she was stuck fast. Releasing her required the manager and a special turnstile key.

Have you ever been trapped with no hope for escape? Held in slavery and in need of salvation? Just like Sarah's turnstile prison, we've all been caught fast in sin with no way to save ourselves. Yet, while we were still held captive God chose to free us and make us His own. And just like God called the children of Israel to holiness when He delivered them from slavery in Egypt, He's called us to holiness. He still calls all His children to holiness.

Based on what we've learned so far, define your call to holiness?

From Scripture, we've learned that our call to holiness is based on the character of God Himself. God is holy. As His children we are called to conform to His character. "Be holy, because I am holy" (1 Peter 1:16). We've also touched on the blessings associated with holy living (which we will explore a little more in Week Five). However, now let's consider another powerful motivation.

Read the Scripture references listed on the left and draw a line to the appropriate phrase on the right.

Galatians 1:3–4   Jesus suffered to make us holy through His blood.

Ephesians 5:25–26   Christ's sacrifice makes us holy.

Hebrews 10:10   Jesus gave Himself for our sins and to rescue us from evil.

Hebrews 13:12   Christ died to make us holy because He loves us.

Based on the verses above, what strong motivation should we have for pursuing holiness?

Jesus died to make us holy. Like the children of Israel, we have gone from chains to chosen to covenant. God chose us to be His own and saved us from the bondage of sin and death. He brought us into the new covenant sealed with the blood of Christ and calls us to respond with holiness.

Read 1 Peter 1:3–4 below. Circle the words that describe the salvation that is ours in Christ.

> *Praise be to the God and Father of our Lord Jesus Christ! In his great mercy he has given us new birth into a living hope through the resurrection of Jesus Christ from the dead, and into an inheritance that can never perish, spoil or fade. This inheritance is kept in heaven for you.*

Read 1 Peter 1:13–16. In light of our salvation, (note the "Therefore" that begins v. 13) how should we respond?

In her book, *Holiness: The Heart God Purifies*, Nancy Leigh DeMoss discusses our holiness in light of Jesus' death:

> When we tolerate our sin and refuse to be parted from it, we spurn the love and the grace of Christ; we trample His Cross and count His sacrificial death of no value. Jesus didn't shed His blood so you and I could have a passport to happiness and heaven, while continuing to indulge our lust, anger, and jealousy; our addictions and critical, competitive spirits; our selfishness and pride. His death provides the motivation and the power to say no to sin and yes to holiness in every area of our lives. Jesus died to make us holy, to deliver us from sin. How, then can we carelessly or casually continue to sin against such a Savior?

Have you ever taken the sacrificial death of Christ for granted? I have. Have you ever been guilty of viewing His death as merely a "Get Out of Jail Free" card? (Maybe you didn't do this consciously, but looking back now, perhaps you realize that attitude was revealed in the way you lived.) Have you failed to change the way you live in light of His grace?

As we close today, let's ask God to give us a fuller understanding of the purpose of Christ's death. May our lives be impacted by His truth.

a light in the darkness

Even one life surrendered to live in the light of Christ can impact the darkness. Just ask Nicky Cruz. Born in Puerto Rico in 1938, Nicky was surrounded by the oppressive darkness of the occult. Until his midteens he suffered physical abuse from his witchcraft-practicing parents. At 15, Nicky went to New York to stay with an older brother; by 16 years old, he was the leader of the brutal Mau Maus, a notorious street gang in Brooklyn.

After years of violence, drugs, and arrests, Nicky encountered a preacher named David Wilkerson. Even after being beaten up and having his life threatened by Nicky, Wilkerson persisted in showing him God's love and sharing the life-changing message of Christ. The result—the dramatic conversion of a soul-scarred, ruthless gangster.

In Day 2 of this week we read 1 John 1:5, "God is light; in him there is no darkness at all." John used light as an analogy for God's holiness, and darkness to represent sin and evil. Holiness in God's people attracts others to God like light beckons us to leave the darkness. Before meeting Christ, Nicky Cruz had known only darkness. Then God used David Wilkerson to show him light. Today Nicky Cruz's ministry reaches tens of millions with the light of Christ. When you visit the home page of his ministry's website, the first thing that catches your eye is this statement: "Imagine what would happen if instead of cursing the darkness we invaded it with light." Just imagine.

Does your life point those around you to God? When was the last time the holiness of your life caused a lost friend or neighbor to acknowledge God and praise Him?

Although God called the nation of Israel to be a holy nation, like us, she did not always heed that call. In fact, after centuries of rebellion and idolatry, God brought discipline. In 722 BC, Assyria conquered the kingdom of Israel. Her citizens were dragged into captivity, bringing a permanent end to the Northern Kingdom. Then in 586 BC, after previous deportations of her people, Babylon completely defeated the Southern Kingdom of Judah and took most of the remaining people back to Babylon. But that's not the end of the story. God had eternal purposes for His people.

Read Ezekiel 36:16–21. Why did God exile His people to Babylon?

Based on this passage, how important is God's holy reputation before the people of the world?

How does the behavior of God's people affect God's holy reputation?

Read Ezekiel 36:8–12. What did God plan to do with and for His people whom he had exiled? Check all that apply.
___ Bring them out of exile and back to the Promised Land.
___ Bless the land and cause it to produce bountiful harvests.
___ Increase the number of people and livestock.
___ Rebuild the towns and repair the ruins.
___ Bring prosperity to the people.

Read Ezekiel 36:22–23, 29–32. Why did God say He would do all this? Mark the following statements True or False:
___ For the sake of Israel.
___ For the sake of God's holy name.

_____ To reveal His holiness to the nations.
_____ To bring Israel to repentance.

Read Ezekiel 36:24–32. How would God's holiness be revealed?

The prophet Ezekiel foretold the return of the exiles to Jerusalem. God fulfilled this prophecy beginning in 538 BC when Cyrus, King of Persia, issued an edict allowing the Israelites to return. God disciplined His people because their lack of holiness had caused the nations to scorn God. He led them back from exile to show His holiness to the world. He brought them to repentance and cleansed their lives from impurity. His Spirit moved them to obedience and He blessed them. God's purpose was for the world to notice and give Him glory.

Week 1
Day 5
30

In his commentary on this passage in Ezekiel, Ralph Alexander observes, "The nations would observe this marvelous transformation in Israel and see the Lord as the only gracious and loving God, for Israel was not deserving of restoration."

God still wants to reveal His holiness to the world through the lives of His people. His purposes have not changed.

Read 1 Peter 2:9–12.

List the words found in verse 9 used to describe God's people.

According to the second half of verse 9, why did God choose us and make us holy?

Reread verses 11–12. What will cause the pagans (ungodly) to glorify God?

I've heard numerous nonbelievers say that the biggest reason they don't go to church or seek God is the hypocrisy of the Christians they know. Granted, some use this as an excuse, but I've heard it too many times for it not to include some truth. Believers, we have been chosen by God and called to be holy so we can reveal Him to a lost world. Are our "good lives" causing others to glorify God or are our "sinful desires" profaning His holy name?

✐ Pause for a moment and ask God to show you how your life impacts those around you. What change can you make in your life today that would cause others to glorify God?

Into His Arms! Embracing a Life of Holiness

When my friend Denise was in high school, something happened to convince her that holiness must be a "consistent lifestyle, one that reflects God's character." This event still encourages her to live in a way that points people to Jesus.

Denise became a Christian as a child, so by the time she was a teenager she actively shared her faith with friends. One day at school, Denise and a friend she had been telling about Jesus were standing around chatting with a group. Someone in the group accused Denise of horribly slandering another person. The friend immediately jumped to her defense. "Denise didn't say those things. She doesn't talk like that about people because it's not who she is." The other teenager had recognized consistent, holy behavior in the life of one of God's children. In fact, it impacted her so greatly, she was convinced she could depend on Denise to always behave that way.

Prayerfully think about your own life. Can you agree with the following statements?

Y   N   My life consistently reflects God's character to the people I know and encounter. My family. My friends. My neighbors. My co-workers. Other drivers on the road. The checker at the grocery store. The coach of my child's sports team.

Y   N   If I was accused of manipulating facts at work to make myself look better, other co-workers would come to my defense.

Y   N   If a neighbor on my block heard someone say I was a Christian, they
would not be surprised.

Y   N   I can honestly say my life is pleasing to God.

As we end this week's study, ask God to show you specific areas of your life that do not reflect His holiness. Write whatever He shows you below.

up close and personal

mily Dickinson ranks among the United States' most-loved nineteenth-century poets. A prolific writer, she wrote hundreds of poems and more than 1,000 letters during her relatively short life. Yet, only 11 pieces of Dickinson's writings were published while she was living. And scholars believe even these were printed without her permission.

After Dickinson's death in 1886, her younger sister, Lavinia, began the requested task of destroying letters Dickinson had received from others. While going through her sister's things, Lavinia discovered a large collection of manuscripts the poet had never mentioned. A whole life—mostly unknown—recorded on paper and hidden away.

Her poetry was not the only thing Dickinson kept concealed. Her reclusive nature is as well known as her writings. Although she freely shared her thoughts and feelings on paper, she severely restricted her human connections and interaction, becoming more and more withdrawn over the years. She chose seclusion and anonymity. Only after her death would readers come to know Emily Dickinson.

God does not choose to hide or conceal Himself. He freely makes Himself known and invites us to explore and experience Him in numerous ways.

First, God reveals Himself to every person in a general way through nature. The heavens and the earth testify to the power and majesty of the Creator. God also reveals Himself in a specific way through His written Word. Through the Bible we learn of God's holy character and righteous ways. Finally and most fully, God reveals Himself personally to us through Jesus Christ.

In this week of study, we will explore the various ways God reveals His holy nature to all humanity. His holiness is not hidden. All can experience and enjoy His majestic glory!

creation sings

Before the stars dotted the heavens and the waves crashed on the shore, God existed in all His holiness. Divine, perfect nature witnessed solely by the Triune God Himself. Then He spoke, and His majesty burst forth in visible wonder. He splashed His glory across the skies and spread His power in the ocean depths.

Now all creation lifts a clear, unbroken chorus of praise to its Creator. Since the beginning of time, what has been made testifies to the unlimited power and worthiness of its Maker. Nature beckons us to seek God, bidding us turn our eyes and hearts to the Creator. It is beyond comprehension that this powerful, majestic, holy God desires us to know Him. And yet He does.

Have you heard the songs of praise? Creation summons us to know and worship the Creator. The psalmist David heard and responded. As a shepherd, he spent many nights under the stars with the sheep, where creation's song fostered his own praise.

Read Psalm 19:1–4 from your favorite translation. What verbs did David use to show how creation testifies to God?

 What does creation reveal about the Creator? (See Psalm 19:1–4.)

According to Psalm 19:1, God's *glory* is clearly evident when we gaze at the works of His hands. "Glory," translated from the Hebrew word *kabed*, refers to the visible manifestation of God. According to the *Theological Wordbook of the Old Testament*, "These manifestations are directly related to God's self-disclosure and his intent to dwell among men. As such they are commonly associated with his holiness. God wishes to dwell with men, to have his reality and his splendor known to them."

When Scripture uses the phrase "glory of God," it means God is revealing aspects of His person or divine nature — especially His holiness — in a visible way. For instance, in creation God demonstrates His unlimited power, boundless creativity, and complete sovereignty. We also experience His absolute holiness as the wonder of His works inspire awe and worship to well up within us.

Who hears this glorious testimony? (Mark all that apply.)
___ People of every language.
___ People in every corner of the world.
___ Only those who already know God.

Creation reveals the power and majesty of God. No language difference or cultural barrier can hinder its message. No government or law can silence its voice. The complex beauty of the heavens and the earth reflect the holiness of God to every person, of every language, in every place. Without exception.

Read Psalm 19:4–6.

From the pastures around Bethlehem, David often witnessed the rising and setting of the sun. Although he did not know then all we know about our star today, David knew God established its impressive course.

What are some things in nature that quickly draw your thoughts to the Creator and initiate praise? What are some ways you can purposefully foster praise?

Creation provides solid evidence of the existence of the Creator. Its beauty and scope demonstrate some of His attributes. Biblical scholars refer to this as natural or general revelation.

Wayne Grudem defines *general revelation*, in his book *Systematic Theology*, "General revelation comes through observing nature, through seeing God's directing influence in history, and through an inner sense of God's existence and his laws that he has placed inside every person."

Through what God has made, all people can know He exists. All people can begin to get a sense of His holy nature. This truth led Paul to conclude that people have no excuse for rejecting the existence and holiness of God.

Read Romans 1:18–23 from the New Living Translation:

But God shows his anger from heaven against all sinful, wicked people who suppress the truth by their wickedness. They know the truth about God because he has made it obvious to them. For ever since the world was created, people have seen the earth and sky. Through everything God made, they can clearly see his invisible qualities — his eternal power and divine nature. So they have no excuse for not knowing God.

Yes, they knew God, but they wouldn't worship him as God or even give him thanks. And they began to think up foolish ideas of what God was like. As a result, their minds became dark and confused. Claiming to be wise, they instead became utter fools. And instead of worshiping the glorious, ever-living God, they worshiped idols made to look like mere people and birds and animals and reptiles.

According to Romans 1:20, what does creation clearly make known about God?

Think specifically for a moment. Contemplate the scope of creation. What qualities or attributes of God are clearly evident?

In this passage, we see two possible responses to creation's testimony. Use Romans 1:18–23 to describe each response in the table below.

Proper Response	Rebellious Response

Week 2
Day 1
37

In Romans 1, Paul emphasizes that sin blinds us to God's glory displayed in creation. Instead of accepting the testimony and worshipping the Creator, people "suppress the truth." The result is idolatry. Since God designed humankind for worship, if we do not worship *Him*, we will find a substitute.

Our "idols" today are rarely literal carved images made from wood, stone, or metal. Anything can become an idol if we give it God's rightful place in our lives.

List some things people worship other than God. Have you ever been guilty of idolatry?

People who ignore nature's testimony and reject God claim to be "wise." In fact, some of the most "scholarly" in our society claim to be atheists. They even attempt to use creation to prove a Creator does not exist. Yet, according to the Bible, their wisdom is most foolish and their godless pursuits futile.

Thankfully, all scientists do not agree on how the universe began and developed. While some insist on a purely natural cause, ruling out the possibility of the divine, others—and yes, there are many—acknowledge that the theory of evolution is insufficient to explain the complexity of our universe. Still others go further and recognize the necessity of an Intelligent Designer. Renowned scientists from fields such as genetics, biology, chemistry, geology, physics, and astronomy, see the glory of God manifest in His creation.

Before we end today, let's allow God's creation to do a little testifying. As you read the following paragraphs, reflect on what these aspects of nature reveal about our great God.

Have you ever stopped to consider the size of the universe? Earth, our home, and seven other planets revolve around a sun to form a single solar system. Yet, our sun is just one of more than 200 billion stars in the Milky Way galaxy. That's big! In fact, it would take us 100,000 years to cross our galaxy at the speed of light. And that's just the beginning. Our galaxy is only one of billions of galaxies across the vast expanse of the cosmos. And our God made it all.

Let's take an abrupt shift in our thinking and move from big to small, from inconceivably huge to microscopically tiny. About 100 trillion cells comprise the human body—including yours. Each cell is packed with DNA. This complex molecule stores information that determines your body's unique physical characteristics, like the color of your eyes. If the DNA in just one cell were laid out flat in one long line, it would stretch more than six feet in length.

The same God who tossed billions of galaxies across the universe also folded six feet of DNA into every cell of your body. He determined the size of the cosmos and counted the number of hairs on your head. The heavens declare the glory of God!

Time to do a little declaring of our own. In the space below, write a prayer of praise and thanksgiving to the Creator.

day two

formal introduction

I took a big step a few months ago. For better or worse, I replaced my old PC with a Mac. I had heard about a Mac's great capability and ease of use, but I knew little. The first day I opened it up and turned it on, pretty much all I could do was admire it. But when I read and followed the instructions about setup and watched some of the tutorials online, I began to understand how to use it. The other day, I even went to the Apple Store for some individual instruction on iMovie. I feel a blockbuster coming on.

Admiring my new laptop was nice, but it didn't get me very far. It simply fostered a desire to learn more, to explore its capabilities. Yesterday, we learned creation reveals God in a limited way. The heavens and earth and all that is in them prove the presence of a Creator and demonstrate many of His attributes. And while this testimony is grand, it's also insufficient for knowing God in a personal way.

According to Romans 1, creation leaves humankind without excuse regarding God's existence and His worthiness to be worshipped. His existence and holy power are obvious to all. But this is just the starting point. God calls us to seek Him and know Him more fully. But, we need more than the general revelation found in creation.

Today, we will witness how God revealed His holiness to the nation of Israel in a very dramatic way and discover what we can learn from their encounter. But first, let's consider God's *special* or *specific* revelation to us through His written Word. The Bible discloses truth about God's character, His will, His ways, and His purposes for us. We need His specific revelation for the gospel message, to know how to live a life that pleases Him, to grow in an intimate relationship with Him, and much more.

The Scriptures below are a small sample of what we can learn about God from His Word. Draw lines to match each passage to what they reveal about our Creator.

Psalm 32:5–22	God's omnipresence
Psalm 119:105	God's plan of salvation
Jeremiah 23:23–24	God's spiritual refinement
John 3:16	God's character
Acts 17:26–27	God's direction
Romans 10:17	God's love
2 Timothy 3:16–17	God's sovereignty
Hebrews 4:12	God's spiritual growth and preparation

Before God's children had His written Word, He appeared or spoke to them on specific occasions and in various ways. Sometimes He communicated something He was about to do. For instance in Genesis 6, God revealed His coming judgment to Noah and included him in His plans. God appeared to Abraham multiple times for different purposes — to give a call, to establish His covenant, to make a promise, to disclose His plans, to put to the test.

Examples of God's personal revelation to His children fill the Old Testament. Through angels, dreams, visions, and theophanies (physical appearance of God to a person), God made Himself, His ways, His purposes, and His plans known to humans.

Perhaps the most dramatic visible revelation of God to His people is found in Exodus 19. Three months after God delivered the children of Israel from slavery in Egypt, He appeared to them on Mount Sinai. He had a specific purpose in mind for this divine encounter. Scripture tells us why God chose to reveal Himself to Israel in this way, at this time. Let's walk through some passages and put the pieces together.

Read Exodus 19:1–6. (This passage is a review from last week to help set the context for the larger passage.) What three descriptive phrases in verses 5–6 describe God's overall plan for the nation of Israel?

God rescued Israel from Egypt and made her His own treasure for a specific purpose. He intended to shape Israel into a nation that would make God and His salvation known to the rest of the world. This "kingdom of priests" was to be a "light for the Gentiles" (Isaiah 49:6), a mediator between God and sinful humanity. What a glorious privilege!

According to Exodus 19:5, what condition must Israel meet to be used by God in this way? (Mark one.)
____ Full obedience.
____ Get a seminary education.
____ Become a world superpower.

God required obedience from His chosen people. In order for God's messengers to the world to be useful in His kingdom, they had to follow His way and not their own. Just like rebellious children don't represent their fathers well, rebellious "priests" cannot adequately represent God to the nations.

For a moment, jump to the end of God's visit to Mount Sinai and read Exodus 20:18–20. Why did God introduce Himself to the people of Israel in such a dramatic way? (Mark all that apply.)
____ To test them.
____ To instill godly fear.
____ To foster obedience.

If Israel obeyed God, He would be able to use them the way He desired — as a beacon to the world. If they remained obedient, if they lived holy lives that reflected God's holiness to the world, they would be a "kingdom of priests" pointing the nations to the one true God. Additionally, they would experience the overwhelming blessing of being God's "treasured possession."

Read Exodus 19:10–25. List the ways God visibly displayed His holiness to Israel.

Look back at verse 16. How did the people respond to God's holy presence? What do you think this physical response implies about their inward spiritual response?

Unfortunately, Israel's obedient response to God's holiness was neither full nor permanent. Exodus and Numbers record multiple occasions of rebellion, idolatry, and grumbling against God as He led them through the wilderness toward the Promised Land. Their disobedience cost them a 40-year delay. Forty years of homelessness. Forty years of wandering and waiting.

But our holy God is merciful and gracious. Although He disciplined Israel for their disobedience, He still longed to bless them and use them to fulfill His purposes. When their time of discipline was complete, He turned them once again toward the land He'd promised. As they prepared to enter and take the land, Moses reminded them of all God had done and wanted to do. (The Book of Deuteronomy records these things.)

Read Deuteronomy 6:1–3. What would be the results of Israel's obedience to God?

Our holy God deserves the awe, reverence, and fear of His people today. When we begin to recognize the depth of His holiness, we will respond with obedience. And obedience brings blessing.

Have you ever had a Mount Sinai experience? A moment when you were overwhelmed by God's holiness? Has He ever revealed Himself to you in a way that caused you to tremble or brought you to your knees?

As we close today, describe that experience below and ask God to refresh your awareness of His holiness. How did you respond? If you have never encountered God in this way, ask Him to make you sensitive to His presence.

day three:

like Father, like Son

When I first met Becky, I formed an initial view based on limited information. This pretty, petite young woman is married to a sweet, godly man. Becky and Brandon have two young boys that require a lot of energy, time, and love from their mom. So it's good that she loves spending time at home with her family and works hard to meet their needs.

Becky's love for children made it a joy to follow God's lead to minister to them in Sunday School, Vacation Bible School, preschool choir, and a host of other ways. Now Becky serves as the director of preschool and children's ministry at her church. She also uses her musical talent on the church praise team where she sings and plays the violin.

Do you have a picture of Becky in your mind? You'd probably use words such as *fun*, *musical*, *energetic*, *loving*, and *kid-friendly*. That's how I pegged her. Now what if I told you Becky has a degree in criminal justice and worked as a felony probation officer dealing with individuals who had been in prison for serious drug offenses? Would that alter your picture of Becky? It definitely expanded mine. This knowledge opened my eyes to other characteristics I had missed but were there all along—attributes such as strength, determination, confidence, and courage.

My initial view of Becky was lopsided. Limited knowledge skewed my understanding to just one side of this unique woman. Likewise, believers can get a lopsided view of Jesus if we don't consider all the facts. Many Christians stand in awe of the Father, but take Jesus too casually.

Jesus is God with us. He is the glory of God made flesh. Today we will dig into Scripture to get a full, well-rounded understanding of the One who came to earth to reveal God's holiness to the world.

Read the following passages. Briefly describe what each one reveals about Jesus' nature, character, authority, or power.
Matthew 11:28–30

Mark 10:13–16

Luke 6:27–36

John 11:32–37

Matthew 26:47–54

Mark 4:35–41

Luke 4:31–37

John 2:13–17

John 11:41–44

This small sample of passages gives us a broad perspective of the person of Christ — from the humble servant who holds a young child on His lap to the zealous Son who physically clears the greedy from His Father's house — they all help us understand who Jesus is.

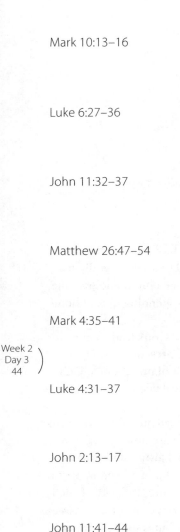 Did anything you discover in the passages above surprise you? If so, what was it?

Let's consider one more vital truth as we work to deepen our understanding of Jesus. Read 2 Corinthians 5:21; Hebrews 4:15; and 1 John 3:5. What common fact do all these verses teach about Jesus?

In Week 1, we defined *holy* as being "morally blameless" and completely "separated from sin." Based on the verses we just read, the Bible clearly teaches that Jesus is holy, just like His Father. Yet sometimes, believers impose a distinction between the Father and Son Scripture does not show. We see the Father as the holy, fear-inspiring God of the Old Testament and Jesus as the grace-filled Savior of the New Testament.

We easily envision the Father as the righteous judge, the one who disciplines, and wields authority. And while true, Scripture also describes Him as our place of refuge and safety, a loving Father who gathers His children under His wings for protection.

In contrast, we tend to "soften" Jesus. We quickly accept Him as the Good Shepherd, but forget He will return soon to judge the world and put all His enemies under His feet. Jesus is both the Good Shepherd and the Rider on the white horse, as described in the Book of Revelation. He is both merciful and righteous. Compassionate and just. Gentle and powerful. He submitted Himself in full obedience to the Father's will, and yet, He has authority over nature and demons and death.

The Father and the Son are two distinct Persons, but they also share one divine nature. The Father and the Son are both holy God. We can understand this truth better by considering what Jesus said about the relationship between Himself and the Father.

Read the following passages and draw a line to the corresponding truth.

John 1:18   The Father makes Himself known through the Son.

John 1:18   The Father is in the Son and the Son is in the Father.

John 10:30   Knowledge of the Son is knowledge of the Father.

John 14:7   The Father and Son are one.

John 14:11   Everything that belongs to the Father belongs to the
                         Son.

John 16:15   The Son reveals the Father.

🗝 Write a summary statement about the relationship between the Father
and the Son.

🗝 Read each passage below. Summarize what you learn about Jesus' divine
nature and His mission to reveal God to the world.

John 1:14–18

Ephesians 1:22–23

Colossians 1:15–20

Our Holy God reveals Himself to us in creation, through His Word, and
ultimately through His Son, Jesus. Jesus is holy God come to us. A revelation to grasp. An example to follow. Our God to worship.

 Did you learn anything today about Jesus that will change the way you relate to Him? If so, what was it and how will it affect your relationship?

As we close today, spend a few moments praising Jesus for who He is and basking in His holiness.

In his book, *The Holiness of God*, R. C. Sproul writes about Moses' desire:

> Moses had been an eyewitness of astonishing miracles. He had heard the voice of God speaking to him out of the burning bush. He had witnessed the river Nile turn into blood. He had tasted manna from heaven and had gazed upon the pillar of cloud and the pillar of fire. He had seen the chariots of Pharaoh inundated by the waves of the Red Sea. Still he was not satisfied. He wanted more. He craved the ultimate spiritual experience. He inquired of the Lord on the mountain, "Let me see your face. Show me your glory."

How did God respond to Moses' request? Mark the one that best describes God's answer.

___ "Get ready! I'm going to give you everything I've got!"

___ "Nope, sorry. You know enough about Me already."

___ "I will show you more of who I am, but for your safety I cannot reveal everything."

Moses desired a deeper, more intimate knowledge of God. He longed to see His holy character displayed in all its fullness. So Israel's leader asked the Creator to show him His glory. But Moses didn't really understand his own request. He didn't realize the potential danger. Unprotected, sinful humanity is not safe in the presence of our holy God.

God told Moses, "You cannot see my face, for no one may see me and live." Based on what you've learned about God's holiness and what you know about the nature of man, explain this statement.

In order to spare Moses' life, God did not completely unveil His holiness. Instead, He took precautions and revealed only as much as Moses could safely receive. R. C. Sproul helps us understand:

> Humans are not allowed to see the face of God. The Scriptures warn that no person can see God and live. . . . God allowed Moses to see His hindquarters but never His face. . . . It is our impurity that prevents us from seeing God. The problem is not with our eyes; it is with our hearts. Only

after we are purified and sanctified in heaven will we have the capacity to gaze upon Him face-to-face.

Seeing God in all His glory would have meant a death sentence for Moses, for he was not without sin. However, because Moses "pleased" God (Exodus 33:17), He honored his request as much as possible.

Read Exodus 33:18–23 and 34:4–8 (Note that 34:4–8 is the fulfillment of God's promise to Moses in 33:19.) What did God do to protect Moses?

List everything God revealed to Moses about Himself.

In addition to revealing specific traits to Moses, God proclaimed His name, the LORD. In ancient times, someone's "name" represented their character, who they were as a person. When God proclaimed His name to Moses, He revealed His divine nature.

"LORD" in Exodus 33:19 and 34:6 is the Hebrew name Yahweh or Jehovah. This is God's personal name, His covenant name. It's also the one God introduced to Moses when He spoke to him from a burning bush in Exodus 3. (Note: Whenever you see LORD in all caps in your Bible, it is Jehovah.) God reveals Himself most uniquely as Jehovah, the God who is self-existent and self-sufficient. Jehovah is the God of covenant who provides a way of salvation for His people.

Moses' encounter with God's holiness had both spiritual and physical affects. Read Exodus 34:29–32. What was the physical effect?

Why do you think the people were afraid to come near Moses?

Moses had indeed been dangerously close to God! His face still reflected God's radiant glory. Moses had basked in the glow of Jehovah's presence and it showed. But the people were afraid. Even God's reflected glory caused them to draw back, to put distance between themselves and the effects of God's presence seen on the face of Moses.

What a contrast! Moses begged to see more of God's holiness. He was willing to risk it all to know more of God. But the Israelites preferred the safety of the status quo. Drawing close would require a drastic change of heart. That was too hard, risky even. They would simply stay at a distance.

As you and I draw closer to our holy God, He will likely show us areas of our life that contradict His holiness. If we want to experience increasingly more of Him we will need to obediently bring our lives in line with His. Then like Moses, the closer we draw to God, the more we experience of His holiness, the more we will reflect His holiness to a watching world.

What about you? Is your desire for more of God stronger than your fear of change? What do you fear God may ask of you?

Tomorrow, we will take the first steps to prepare ourselves to encounter our holy God. But as we close today, write a request to God. Voice your desire to see His glory!

better get ready!

In the classic book *The Lion, the Witch and the Wardrobe* by C. S. Lewis, four children step through a wardrobe into the magical land of Narnia. They discover that the evil White Witch holds Narnia in her powerful grasp and its inhabitants have almost lost hope. But just in time, Aslan the lion returns and provides salvation through a great sacrifice.

Sound familiar? Lewis intentionally patterned his character Aslan after Christ. When Mr. and Mrs. Beaver told the children about Aslan, Susan asked if the lion was "safe." Mr. Beaver responded, "Who said anything about safe? 'Course he isn't safe. But he's good. He's the King, I tell you."

God is not safe, but He is good. Do you want to know God more? To experience Him in a deeper way than you do now? He wants to make Himself known to us, to reveal His holiness. But before we ask Him to show us His glory, we should consider some preparations.

In his book, *The Knowledge of the Holy*, A. W. Tozer tells readers we can deepen our knowledge of a holy God: "God is a Person and can be known in increasing degrees of intimate acquaintance as we prepare our hearts for the wonder." But he also elaborates on certain "conditions" necessary for believers to draw close to the "Majesty in heaven."

The first condition Tozer cites is the need to forsake sin. A holy God "cannot be known by men of confirmed evil lives." We explored this truth a bit yesterday when we studied Moses' request to see God's glory. Other passages in the Bible also teach this truth.

Read the following passages and describe the connection between forsaking sin and drawing close to our holy God.

Psalm 24:2–4

Matthew 5:8

Hebrews 12:14

🗝 Based on what you've learned so far about God's holiness, why do you think we need genuine repentance and a commitment to obedience to grow in our knowledge of God?

Today we will spend some time in honest, personal reflection to prepare ourselves to encounter God. But first let's look back at God's visit to the people of Israel at Mount Sinai we explored on Day 2 of this week. God gave Moses specific instructions for the people to prepare themselves.

Read Exodus 19:9–25. What preparations did the people undergo before they could meet with God (see vv. 10–15)?

The Lord told Moses to consecrate the people. OK, but what does that mean? Interestingly, the Hebrew word translated as "consecrate" or "sanc-tify" is the verb form of the adjective holy we defined earlier. (See Week 1, Day 2.) *The Complete Word Study Old Testament* defines the verb as "to make clean; dedicate to God; treat as holy; to purify, make oneself clean; to seclude."

I found this further explanation especially helpful:

> This verb captures the element of being pure or devoted to God. (It) signifies an act or a state in which people or things are set aside for use in the worship of God. . . . They must be withheld from ordinary use and treated with special care as something which belongs to God. Otherwise defilement makes the sanctified object unusable.

✎ Using the definition for *consecrate* and the information in Exodus 19:9–25, write a conclusion about God's intention for telling the people to consecrate themselves.

God wanted His people in the right condition to worship when He met with them. The proper and natural response of a pure heart to our holy God is worship. Worship draws us close. Worship fosters intimacy. Worship forges bonds. But sin dampens worship. That's why Israel needed consecration. That's why we need consecration.

Similar commands from God to His children fill the New Testament as well. For instance, "Make every effort to live in peace with everyone and to be holy; without holiness no one will see the Lord" (Hebrews 12:14). Other translations use "strive for" and "pursue."

These commands imply that consecration—or holiness—does not simply happen naturally on it's own when we become a Christian. We must be purposeful and diligent in pursuing a life of holiness. In her book, *Holiness: The Heart God Purifies*, author Nancy Leigh DeMoss writes about this purposeful pathway to holiness:

> I think deep down we'd like to find a pathway to sanctification that is instant and effortless—no long process, no hard battle. The fact is, there is no such thing. According to Hebrews 12:14, the pathway of holiness requires intensity and intentionality. . . . In other words, we must make it our constant, conscious ambition and aim to be holy. We have to work at it, concentrate on it, as an athlete sets his sights on winning an Olympic medal: He focuses on his objective, he trains and strains to achieve his goal, he sacrifices for it, he endures pain for it, and he puts aside other pursuits for the sake of a higher pursuit."

"Strive." "Pursue." "Make every effort." Although God alone can purify our hearts and minds, He demands our obedient cooperation. As we diligently pursue holiness in concrete ways, God will do the spiritual work within us. Israel's acts of consecration did not prepare their hearts to meet with God, but God did work through their obedience to purify them.

In what ways do you think God used Israel's obedient acts of clothes washing and sexual abstinence to prepare them spiritually to meet with Him? (See Exodus 19.)

Although not explained in the passage, we can make some educated assumptions about the value of the clothes washing and sexual abstinence. The act of washing physically demonstrates what needs to happen spiritually before we approach God. This "cleansing" is part of the consecration process, ridding our hearts and minds of sin and rebellion. Abstaining from sex for a limited period of time — or anything else that distracts us — helps us focus on pleasing God and connecting with Him in worship.

Think about your own life. What are some things that consume a lot of your time and energy?

Do these things tend to draw your focus away from God? How would you feel about abstaining from them for a limited period of time to concentrate on Him?

List anything else you think could be part of a spiritual consecration process. (For instance, I would put prayer and repentance on my list.)

Throughout our study together, we will have opportunities to purposefully pursue holiness. Our goal is to draw ever closer to God as we obediently allow Him to consecrate our lives. As we close today, let's take a few moments to prepare our hearts.

Read Psalm 139:23–24, printed below, as a prayer to God. Invite God to search your heart and mind for anxious thoughts, selfish motivations, sinful habits, and rebellious ways. Write down whatever He brings to mind. Ask Him to help you obey Him and diligently strive for holiness.

> Search me, O God, and know my heart; test me and know my
> anxious thoughts. Point out anything in me that offends you,
> and lead me along the path of everlasting life.

(PSALM 139:23–24 NLT)

Lisa had longed to see Old Faithful since she studied the geyser in her sixth grade geography class. Artesian springs were abundant around her southeast Texas home, but their gently flowing waters could not satisfy her desire to witness the power of Yellowstone National Park's most famous natural site.

Unfortunately, Lisa's family did not have the resources for many vacations, so almost three decades passed before she stood on the viewing platform next to Old Faithful. Lisa, her husband, and their five children had started their trip at the northern end of the park. They enjoyed the hot springs, canyon, mud pots, and wild life. But she purposefully saved the geyser for last.

Lisa knew the geyser would be impressive, but the depth of her reaction surprised her. The eruption built until water and steam reached more than 150 feet into the air. The power of nature demonstrated by the Old Faithful geyser turned Lisa's heart and mind to the power of its Creator. The holiness of God overwhelmed her as she witnessed His majesty revealed in His creation.

"All I could think of was the majesty of God; how holy and mighty beyond my imagination. He had created this spectacular display of power, yet it is miniscule compared to God's power. I could stand safely on the viewing platform and witness the power of the geyser, but I knew I could never stand in the presence of God except by His grace through Christ. I worshipped God in that moment. He had given me a glimpse of His majesty."

What are a few things in nature that strike you as particularly beautiful, powerful, or majestic?

Have you ever had an experience like Lisa's, a time when God's creation prompted spontaneous worship of Him? If so, describe it briefly.

If not, what can you do to purposefully respond with worship when you witness God's glory in His creation?

As we close this week, call to mind something in creation that mightily demonstrates God's power and holiness. Write a prayer of praise and worship to its Creator.

face-to-face

The power of the ocean surprised me. I had heard stories of rogue waves, dangerous currents, and destructive tsunamis, but I had never experienced them. That was before the Pacific caught me in its pull.

Our family was vacationing on the Hawaiian island of Kauai. We rented boogie boards earlier in the day, and I eagerly wanted to try mine out. When we hit the beach, I didn't hesitate. I jumped right in and paddled out to catch the waves. Unfortunately, by the time I realized they were breaking too far out for boogie boarding, I was in over my head. So with my upper body on the small board, I began to kick my way back to the beach.

Despite my efforts I couldn't make any progress. In fact, after several minutes of trying I was farther away from the beach and farther down the shoreline. The board was strapped to my wrist so I let it trail behind me and began to swim. I swam until I was exhausted and swallowing water, but I was even farther from shore.

Powerless against the riptide, all I could do was cling to the board and yell for help. My dear husband, who came quickly to my side atop his own boogie board, talked me through riding out the current. Soon we were safely on the beach.

That experience gave me new respect for the ocean. Without firsthand knowledge of its power, I had treated the water too casually. My new attitude does not prevent me from enjoying the ocean, but I approach it differently than I did before. The personal encounter with its power changed everything.

Likewise, intellectual assent to the holiness of God is not the same as personal experience. We can mentally agree to the truth that God is holy, but when we come face to face with His holiness, we are forced to respond.

But how will we respond? Will it be in the way God deserves? I hope we will respond in a way that will deepen and strengthen our relationship with Him.

Last week we prepared our hearts to meet with God, to come face-to-face with His holiness. This week we will consider the proper response by examining a few positive and negative examples from Scripture. I pray we will learn to respond to our holy God in the way He deserves. May the experience of His holiness draw us closer into His loving embrace.

go away (fear, hate, and rejection)

One week ago today, on May 20, 2013, a tornado ripped through Moore, Oklahoma. This powerful funnel cloud tore through schools, businesses, and the hospital. It killed 24 people and left thousands homeless. The tornado, with winds exceeding 200 mph, was given an EF5 rating, the strongest ranking possible. This rare twister left a path of destruction 17 miles long and almost 1½ miles wide. Powerful and destructive.

Today, we will witness Jesus' power—not destructive power—but power of authority. His power is mightier than any tornado or army. Stronger than any natural or supernatural force. Through this display of power, Jesus revealed His holiness to His disciples, a demon-possessed man, and a whole town. Let's see how they responded.

Read Mark 4:35–41. (We also read this story last week in a list of passages proving Jesus' deity.)

It had been a long day in Galilee. The people kept coming, and Jesus kept teaching. But when evening fell, Jesus and His disciples climbed into boats and headed across the unpredictable Sea of Galilee.

Briefly describe what happened on the lake.

How did the disciples respond to Jesus' demonstrated authority over nature?
____ They worshipped Jesus.
____ They were terrified and wondered how Jesus could command the storm.
____ They high-fived each other and slapped Jesus on the back.

In his book, *The Holiness of God*, R. C. Sproul reflects on the disciples' response:

> What is significant about this scriptural story is that the disciples' fear increased after the threat of the storm was removed. The storm had made them afraid. Jesus' action to still the tempest made them more afraid. In the power of Christ they met something more frightening than they had ever met in nature. They were in the presence of the holy.

Why do you think the holy power of Jesus frightened them more than the very real threat of drowning?

This display of Jesus' holy power flows immediately into another. Still reeling from Jesus' effective rebuke of a deadly storm, the disciples witnessed Jesus' power over the spiritual world.

Week 3
Day 1
60

The following story is one of my favorites in Scripture. It reveals so much about Jesus' nature and character. We see His compassion, but it's His power over evil that so captures my attention. Even a legion of demons is no match for the Son of God!

Read Mark 5:1–20. Describe the man who ran to meet Jesus on the shore. What was his situation?

Jesus and His disciples sailed from Galilee, crossed the lake in a storm, and arrived on the eastern side probably well after dark. The region was home to ten Gentile cities known as the Decapolis, so the man Jesus encountered was not Jewish.

Did you sense the battle raging inside this desperate individual? He lived among the dead, isolated from other humans, yet the demons overwhelmed him. They called themselves Legion. Since more than 6,000 soldiers comprise a legion, clearly a horde of demons had taken up residence in this man.

Even though there's power in numbers, even thousands of evil spirits were no match for the divine. The Holy elicited an immediate response from the unholy. They recognized Jesus and acknowledged His power.

They even begged Him for mercy. Jesus' power and authority over these demons proved His deity and demonstrated His holiness.

The disciples' reaction to Jesus' new display of power is not mentioned in this story. Recall how they reacted after Jesus calmed the storm. How do you think they may have reacted to this display of power?

Look back at the description you wrote of the demon-possessed man. Now write a description of the man after Jesus freed him from the legion of demons.

When Jesus sent the demons into the nearby herd of pigs, the 2,000 crazed swine rushed into the lake and drowned. The people tending the pigs ran to town with a full report and soon the locals came out to see for themselves.

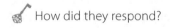 How would you expect the local people to respond when they saw the effect of Jesus' power?

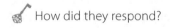 How did they respond?

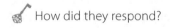 Why do you think they responded this way? (Mark all that apply.)
____ They feared Jesus' power because they weren't sure where it came from.
____ They were worried how their lives might change if they accepted Jesus as God.
____ They were upset that Jesus' actions had cost them financially.

 What other reason might have caused them to respond as they did?

The Son of God demonstrated His holiness by overpowering a legion of demons and restoring a man who had been in spiritual bondage. While the freed man longed to follow Jesus, everyone else ran Him out of town. Why such a difference in responses? It's a matter of the heart.

We see another response similar to these townspeople in a story told in Acts 16. In the name and power of Jesus, Paul exorcised a demon from a slave girl in Philippi.

Read Acts 16:16–24. Why were the slave owners so upset when Paul freed the girl from the demon? What similarities do you see with the story in Mark 5?

Week 3
Day 1
62

In Week 1, I told you about Nicky Cruz, the violent gang member turned evangelist. Jesus' encounter with Legion reminded me of the first time Nicky met David Wilkerson, the preacher who introduced him to Christ. Nicky shared the encounter in his book, *Run Baby Run*.

Wilkerson, a preacher from Pennsylvania, held a youth rally on the street in the Mau Maus' Brooklyn turf on a hot afternoon in the summer of 1958. Standing on a piano bench to be seen by those gathered, Wilkerson read John 3:16 from the huge black Bible in his hands. He told the crowd of gang members that Jesus loved them. Nicky recalls shaking with fear. "I began to sense that this man was dangerous. He was invading our world and I didn't want any strangers intruding." Nicky didn't know how to deal with his fear. It overwhelmed him, pushed him close to panic, and manifested itself as hate.

After the rally, Wilkerson showed up at the Mau Maus' hangout to talk to Nicky. But before Wilkerson could finish a sentence, Nicky slapped him across the face and spit on him. Nicky pushed him and insisted he leave. "Nicky, before I leave let me tell you just one thing. Jesus loves you." "Get out, you crazy priest. You don't know what you're talking about. I'll give you 24 hours to get off my turf or I'll kill you." Although Nicky acted out with hatred and violence, in reality he felt desperate and completely undone. Deep inside, Nicky knew David Wilkerson had something real.

Nicky Cruz felt threatened. Not by Wilkerson, but by the truth of Christ he preached. The townspeople in Mark 5 and the slave owners in Acts 16 also felt threatened by Jesus' power and holiness. Like Nicky, they responded with fear, rejection, and hate.

What do you think is the underlying cause of this kind of response to the holiness of Jesus?

Do people still respond to Christ in this way? If so, give an example.

As we close today, ask God to show you if you ever respond to Christ—even in a minor way—with fear, rejection, or hate. If so, ask God to change your attitudes and motivations that cause you to respond this way.

better get busy

How do you usually answer this question, "How are you?" Many, if not most of you, probably answered with something like this: "Fine, busy." I hear it every day, sometimes out of my own mouth. It seems we can't be "fine" unless we're also busy. Our culture puts high value on doing — pushing us to be everything, do everything, and see everything.

We have been trained to "do." This conditioning makes it difficult for us to be still. Quiet tends to unnerve us. Psalm 46:10 causes us to break out in a cold sweat. "What? I don't have time to be still and know that God is God. There are just too many things on my to-do list."

We see busyness as productive and positive and sitting still and "doing nothing" as a waste of valuable time. Yet, our constant state of doing prevents us from truly experiencing God in all His holiness. No time remains to soak in His presence. No time remains to sit still before God. No time remains to develop deep intimacy with the only One who can meet our every need.

Actually, this human problem is not new. The infamous hostess Martha couldn't slow down long enough to join her sister at the feet of Jesus (Luke 10:38–42). And my favorite apostle, Peter, could not simply bask in the glory of the unveiled Jesus on the Mount of Transfiguration. He felt the need to do something.

Read Matthew 17:1–9.

Jesus brought Peter, James, and John with Him up the mountain to observe a miraculous transformation. The Greek verb, translated as "transfigured" in Matthew 17:2, is *metamorphoo*. According to *The Complete Word Study New Testament*, edited by Spiros Zodhiates, *metamorphoo* denotes a "change of condition, to form." And these three alone were invited to see Jesus' glorious metamorphosis.

Describe Jesus' glorified appearance.

Jesus laid down the dullness of humanity so the glory of His holiness could shine through. The majesty of God displayed for three Galilean fishermen. You think they'd be awestruck. Speechless. On their faces. But instead, Peter opens his mouth and jumps in like a preschooler interrupting his father in an important meeting.

 Briefly summarize how Peter responded to Jesus' revealed holiness.

How did God the Father respond?

We don't know the thoughts that drove Peter's suggestion, but he obviously did not fully grasp the situation. When he should have been still and silent, he was moving and talking. His default setting was to do something. Peter was probably already gathering wood when the Father broke in and stopped him in his busy, little tracks. Clearly Peter was moved, but his response was impulsive and quickly rebuked by God the Father.

Even though the Father appeared to chastise Peter, I love that two members of the Trinity displayed their glory on the mountain. God the Father enveloped them in a "bright cloud" (Matthew 17:5). According to Vine's Complete Expository Dictionary, the Greek word translated as "bright" means "full of light." The Father did not manifest His glory as a dark, brooding storm cloud, but a radiant cover composed of light.

Here on the mountain, Peter, James, and John witnessed glory upon glory. They were enveloped by the Father's shining presence and caught a momentary falling away of Jesus' humanity. They were privileged to glimpse the Son's preincarnate glory, the holiness of Christ displayed to common sinners. The text even suggests this was the purpose of the event: for Peter, James, and John to experience the holiness of Christ.

What are some reasons you can think of that would make this experience necessary for Peter, James, and John?

Peter's immediate response to the revealed glory of Christ was not quite what it could have been. However, the experience continued to impact him and the others. After the Resurrection, all these men fully committed themselves to follow Christ, no matter where He led or what the consequences. For all of them, it meant hardship and persecution. For Peter and James, it also meant martyrdom. The revealed glory of Christ on the mountain gave them what they needed to walk this path. Peter even reflected on this experience in his last days.

Read 2 Peter 1:12–18. According to his own retelling, what did Peter witness on the mountain?

What did this experience with the holiness of Christ do for Peter? (Mark all that apply based on this passage.)
____ Confirmed the identity of Jesus.
____ Fostered an unwavering commitment to the gospel message.
____ Eliminated fear of death.

The Apostle John spent a large part of the last decade of his life in exile on Patmos, a small, isolated island off the coast of Asia. Although not martyred, he was banished "because of the word of God and the testimony of Jesus" (Revelation 1:9). While on Patmos, John was granted another experience with the glorified Christ.

Read Revelation 1:9–18. Write a description of Jesus. What similarities do you see with Jesus' description in Matthew 17?

How did John respond to the majesty of Jesus in Revelation 1:17? Why do you think he reacted this way?

Before we rush off into the rest of our day, I'd like for us to consider how to apply what we've learned today. Let's use the experience of Peter, James, and John to evaluate if we're ready to witness His majesty.

If you had been on the mountain, how do you hope you would have responded? How do you think you would have responded?

What comes more naturally to you, sitting quietly and listening to God or doing something for God?

If sitting quietly is difficult, why do you think that is?

How do you think a "doing" nature could hinder intimacy with God?

You can experience our holy God in a real way. For instance, God can reveal His holiness to you when you are enjoying a magnificent sunset or reading His Word and praying. Sometimes we simply don't wait before Him long enough. We see His glory in nature or we read of His majesty in Scripture, pause long enough to say, "Wow," then we're off and running again. I'm guilty of that. What about you?

As we close today, read Revelation 1:12–18 again. Ask Jesus to overwhelm you with His holiness and wait before Him. Let His majesty envelop you like a bright cloud. Now sit, be still, and know.

what was your name again?
(doubt and disobedience)

Sometimes it happens several times a day. The phone rings and when I answer an overly friendly voice says, "Hi, Kathy! How are you? Everything going OK for you today?"

I don't recognize the voice, but he acts like he knows me. So I respond with great hesitancy, "Yes, everything's fine. How are you?" Half of me expects the caller to identify himself as a distant cousin, and the other half predicts it's just another marketing call. Nine and a half times out of ten it's someone who wants my money, my time, or both.

Unfortunately, all those marketers have made me wary and distrustful of calls that come on our landline. If that phone rings, it's usually somebody trying to sell me something I don't need or want. In fact, it seems I answer our landline with a different tone of voice than I do my cell phone. Not long ago I answered a landline call, and it was that half time out of ten. The acquaintance on the other end immediately asked if something was wrong. Uh-oh.

Moses once received a strange call. Although the holy Caller demonstrated power and authority, Moses initially responded with excuses and distrust. Today, we will see another example of an improper response to God's holiness and discover truth we can apply to our own lives.

Read Exodus 3:1–10.

Forty years before this event, Moses had fled Egypt after killing an Egyptian who was beating an Israelite slave. Moses spent those four decades tending sheep for his father-in-law. He knew the desert well and was familiar with its sights. But this day, Moses witnessed something he had never seen before.

What caught Moses' attention and drew him to take a closer look?
___ A cool spring surrounded by palm trees.
___ A bright cloud descending on the mountain.
___ A burning bush that did not burn up.

What two things did God tell Moses to do in verse 5?
1.

2.

More than likely, Mount Horeb is another name for Mount Sinai. This mountain, where God revealed His holiness to Moses, is the same spot where God would reveal Himself to the nation of Israel and give them the Ten Commandments (Exodus 19). No wonder Moses referred to it as the "mountain of God" throughout the Book of Exodus.

The fire that drew Moses symbolizes God's holy presence. The Holy One—the God of Abraham, Isaac, and Jacob—had come to reveal His plan to Moses. First, God initiated the conversation by calling Moses by name. Then God required Moses to do two things to teach him respect for His holiness and to protect Moses from His powerful, holy presence.

How did Moses respond when God identified Himself in Exodus 3:6? Based on his physical response, what do you think Moses was thinking and feeling?

After Moses was prepared, God identified Himself as the God of Moses' ancestors. This knowledge, combined with the visual manifestations of God's presence, moved Moses from casual observer to fearful worshipper. When Moses first approached, he had to be prompted to respond properly to holy God. But after God further revealed Himself, Moses instinctively hid his face. Fearful respect and awe of the Holy One swept over him.

Based on Exodus 3:7–10, what did God plan to do? How did Moses fit into God's plan?

Read Exodus 3:11–4: 17. As you read, fill out the table below. On the left, list every excuse and doubt-filled question of Moses. (You should find at least five!) On the right, record God's response.

Moses' Excuses and Doubts	God's Response

Initially, Moses worshipped God. But when God announced He would be sending Moses to carry out this rescue mission, Moses developed a different attitude. What do you think was behind his excuses and questions? What do they reveal about Moses' heart and mind?

Moses lacked confidence in himself and his ability. The daunting task seemed impossible to him. Moses allowed his feelings about himself to override the truth that this was God's mission to complete. Moses would not have to speak to Pharaoh with his own words. Moses would not have to deliver the people with his own strength. Moses was not responsible for the mission's success.

Moses not only doubted himself, he also doubted God. Just imagine the questions running through his mind. *Will God really go with me? Can God really bring the people out? Does God really know what He's doing?*

Moses' questions reveal he doubted the faithfulness, power, and authority of God. Moses had seen what Pharaoh could do, but he wasn't sure what God could do? God patiently answered Moses' questions and reassured him again and again. Then when Moses ran out of excuses, what was buried under it all came to the surface.

Reread Exodus 4:13. What does this statement reveal about Moses?

"Get somebody else! I don't want to do it!" Can you see Moses digging in his heels? He didn't want to go, no matter what God said. Underneath Moses' excuses was simple disobedience. "Then the LORD's anger burned against Moses" (Exodus 4:14), and the next thing we know Moses is on his way to Egypt.

According to the *Theological Wordbook of the Old Testament*, the Hebrew verb translated as "burned" or "kindled" is related to a rare Aramaic root word meaning "to cause fire to burn" and to an Arabic root meaning "burning sensation." Moses may have seen and felt the flare of God's anger from the fire in the bush.

God's righteous anger is an aspect of His holiness. Because God is holy, He is "totally good and completely without evil." He cannot tolerate sin and rebellion. Therefore, God made it clear He would not tolerate Moses' disobedience. All it took for Moses was a mere brush with God's holy anger and everything changed. Moses responded with obedience to this display of God's holiness.

When was the last time you balked at obeying God?

Did you feel His displeasure? If so, in what way? How can you respond differently next time?

As we close today, ask God to show you any areas of your life where disobedience reigns. Write down these areas. In light of God's holiness, are you willing to submit these areas to Him?

too big for my britches
(humility and repentance)

To celebrate a special occasion, my husband, Wayne, and I attended a dinner and blues concert featuring one of his favorite music artists. I purchased the tickets online and paid a deposit. The balance would be due at the restaurant. We enjoyed the food and loved the music.

When the evening ended, Wayne paid the bill. On the way home I asked about the total, and he handed me the receipt. It was much higher than I expected. When we got home, I compared it to my online receipt and quickly decided we had been overcharged. I went to bed determined to call the next day to ask for a refund.

The next afternoon I made the call. The man who answered identified himself as Brad. He patiently listened to my story and my accusation, and then looked up my purchase. Brad politely asked me to take another look at my receipt to see if the waiter had applied my deposit.

Oops. Right there at the bottom of the previous night's receipt was a credit for the online deposit. I suspect Brad knew all along what I would find when I took another look. The restaurant had handled everything correctly — and kindly. I was in the wrong. I accused them of overcharging me without all the facts.

I apologized multiple times and thanked Brad for his patience. I gushed about what a wonderful time we'd had the night before. Before we ended the phone call, Brad invited Wayne and me to come back as their guests for the next concert. I sure felt foolish. We had been treated fairly from the beginning and got to enjoy another dinner and concert at no cost.

This was not the first time I'd made unjust accusations. In my sinful flesh, I sometimes speak before I thoroughly think through a situation or express my opinion without all the facts. But the Holy Spirit always convicts me. He shows me my sin, guides me to repentance, and prompts me to make things right with the other person.

Job had a similar experience on a much grander scale. In the midst of circumstances he did not understand, he pointed an accusing finger at God. Without all the facts, Job spoke rashly and harshly against the Creator. In today's lesson, we'll see how quickly Job's attitude changed when our holy God made an appearance.

Read Job 1:1–3. This passage describes Job's life before the times of testing. How does the Bible describe Job? What kind of man was he?

Although not perfect, Job had moral and spiritual integrity. He revered God and sought to live a life that pleased Him. Job set an example for his family and pointed them to God. Therefore, Satan didn't like Job very much. He asked God for permission to test him (Job 1:6–12). He wanted to prove Job's faith was superficial and flimsy—that it would crumble when put under pressure. The Lord allowed the testing. Would Job's faith withstand the trials?

Week 3
Day 4
73

Read Job 1:13–22. Job lost his herds, his servants, and his children. According to verses 20–21, what was his response? How did Job feel about God?

Look at verse 22 again. At this point, how is Job standing up to the test? How does the Scripture describe Job's response?

Not satisfied with the results, Satan asked God for permission to increase the pressure on Job. Satan argued that yes, Job stood strong through loss, but if he had to suffer physical affliction, he would certainly curse God. Once again, God allowed trials into Job's life.

Read Job 2:7–10. Describe Job's physical condition.

What new pressure does Job experience from his wife? How did he respond?

We do not have time to explore the nature of suffering or discuss the well-debated question of God's love and sovereignty against the world's evil and humanity's pain. Our purpose today is to study Job's response to ongoing trials and the change in his response when he encounters the holiness of God.

Job essentially lost everything—his possessions and livelihood, his family (except a nagging wife), and his health. Job's friends came to visit and blamed him for his situation. The physical pain, depth of loss, ongoing suffering, and lack of comfort from his friends finally took a toll on Job's faith.

Although Job would not curse God, he did curse the day God gave him life (Job 3:1), calling God's actions into question. This was just the beginning of a string of accusations and misguided assumptions Job hurled

at God.

 Read the following passages and write each of Job's accusations in your own words:

27:2
29:2–3
29:4–5
30:11
30:20
30:21

Job faced great trials. He did not understand why God allowed such suffering into his life. When the terrible circumstances lingered and his friends continued to blame him, Job reached the breaking point. Armed with unjust accusations, he confronted God. Job even demanded that the God of the universe explain Himself. "I sign now my defense—let the Almighty answer me; let my accuser put his indictment in writing" (Job 31:35). And God answered.

 Read Job 38:1–3. What do God's words reveal about Job's accusations?

Just as God spoke to Moses out of the burning bush, He spoke to Job out of a storm. Jehovah chose a "storm" or "whirlwind" to manifest His holy presence to His servant. Job had accused the holy One of unholy actions. He had spoken without sufficient knowledge. Now it was time for God to speak.

Skim Job 38:4–39:30. Consider the following actions. Put a check mark in front of any within God's power. Circle any within Job's power.
_____ Laid the foundations of the earth.
_____ Commands the weather.
_____ Controls the heavenly bodies.
_____ Rules over and provides for the animal kingdom.

God declared His power as Creator and His authority and right to rule all He created. God used multiple examples to prove His point—from the ocean depths to the celestial bodies He is Lord.

Now read Job 40:1–5. Compare 40:2 with 31:35. Did God hear Job's accusations? (Circle one.)

No   Maybe   Definitely

How did Job respond to God's declaration of His power in verses 4–5? Mark any statements below that reflect the feelings behind Job's words.
_____ I am humbled by Your glorious presence.
_____ I should never question Your character.
_____ I will be silent and listen to You.
_____ I still think You have some explaining to do.

God revealed Himself to Job to instruct him in the truth. Job had felt abandoned and attacked by God. But Job's feelings were not accurate. Acting on incorrect feelings and lack of information, Job had accused God of injustice and demanded a response. But God's holy presence caused a complete change of attitude.

After Job's initial response, God spoke again. (See Job 40:6–41:34.) Now God questions Job. "Would you discredit my justice?" (40:8). "Can your voice thunder like his?" (v. 9). "Who has a claim against me that I must pay?" (41:11).

God also speaks of large, powerful animals. Puny Job is no match for the behemoth (40:15) with its "limbs of iron." Yet God controls it easily. Many scholars believe the behemoth is what we know as the hippopotamus. Even this powerful animal submits to God.

I've never come up against a hippo, but we did encounter an angry elephant in South Africa. Our group was driving through Kruger National Park when we came upon a large herd of females and their young crossing the road. One large, irate female was apparently stationed as guard. Each time we tried to pass, she made short charges at our 12-passenger van.

After several attempts and retreats on our part, the elephants finally moved on, and we were able to continue on our way. Even in a large vehicle, we were no match for the three-ton beast. She knew it and we knew it. She could have crushed us like a tin can. But her power is nothing compared to God's.

Read Job's final response to God in 42:1–6.

Job's declaration in verse 5 is telling. Job had heard about God his entire life. He thought he knew a lot, and he had based his accusations on that knowledge. But when Job experienced God—when the Creator revealed His holiness to the created—he realized how wrong his response to God had been.

Based on Job 42:1–6, what did Job learn about God from the encounter?

How did Job respond to this new understanding of our holy God?

Encountering God's holiness did not immediately change Job's circumstances. However, it did change Job's response. Job did not learn why he had to suffer, but he did learn to trust the ever-present God. Job turned his unjust accusations to repentance. Job turned his death wish to worship. Because Job experienced God's holiness, he found rest and comfort in His presence, even in the midst of his suffering.

As we close today, reflect on any times you may have pointed an accusing finger at the Almighty God. Briefly describe those times below. Humbly come to Him in repentance and ask Him to correct your thinking. Journal your thoughts.

i'm speechless (repentance, submission, and obedience)

Over my lifetime, I've spent many hours soaking up the sun. I tan easily and love that golden glow. However, I clocked most of that time before I understood the very real danger of skin cancer.

Even though I can't see it by simply looking in a mirror, no doubt all that sun exposure has damaged my skin. If I really wanted to know the extent of the damage, I could step under an ultraviolet (UV) light. Blemishes and freckles the human eye can't see in normal light would be revealed with the higher-frequency UV light.

You've probably seen some of those dramatic side-by-side photos. A woman's face in normal light compared to her face under UV light. The differences can be shocking. The damage is there all along; we just can't see it under normal light conditions.

Our life is like that. When we compare ourselves to people around us, we look pretty good. We may even look pretty righteous. However, when we compare ourselves to the Holy One, it's a different story. The light of God's holiness reveals our sin like a UV light reveals the blemishes on our skin. No rebellious behavior, wrong motive, or selfish attitude can hide from God's holy brilliance.

God revealed His holiness to the prophet Isaiah. When Isaiah received a deeper understanding of God, he also received a deeper understanding of his own sin. Today we'll take a close look at this glorious encounter and see how Isaiah responded to God's holiness revealed.

Read Isaiah 6:1–8.

Isaiah was God's prophet to the Southern Kingdom of Judah for at least 30 years and possibly as many as 50. He responded to God's dramatic call around 740 BC, "the year that King Uzziah died." God sent Isaiah to call His people to repentance. They worshipped God ritualistically and made the required sacrifices, but their hearts were rebellious and many openly practiced idolatry. Compared to the people, Isaiah was righteous. Then Isaiah encountered the Holy One.

Look back at Isaiah 6:1. What can we learn about God through the description in just this one verse?

In the year the king of Judah died, Isaiah was powerfully reminded the King of kings was still on His throne. Jehovah God has forever and will always reign above any earthly king or ruler.

Who else did Isaiah see in this vision? Describe them.

According to the *Theological Wordbook of the Old Testament*, the word *seraph* is derived from a root word meaning "fire." "These angelic beings were brilliant as flaming fire, symbolic of the purity and power of the heavenly court."

Picture this scene. These dazzling creatures worshipped One much more glorious than they. The seraphim covered their faces to shield them from the transcendent glory of God and covered their feet to demonstrate humility. As they flew they all declared to one another the ultimate holiness of God.

> "Holy, holy, holy is the LORD of Heaven's Armies!
> The whole earth is filled with his glory!"
>
> (ISAIAH 6:3 NLT)

Once was not enough. Twice still could not convey the magnitude of it. But three times makes a point. God is more than holy. He is the epitome of holiness. He is transcendent in His holiness.

The Hebrew adjective translated as "holy" is the same word we defined in Week 1. God is completely free from any moral imperfections or frailties. Because He is holy, He can be counted faithful to keep His promises.

Because He is holy, He opposes sin and evil. Because He is holy, His people cannot worship Him and persist in sin and rebellion.

The word *glory* refers to the manifestation of God's holiness. God's holy presence is not confined to heaven. Our God is everywhere, filling every place with His transcendent holiness.

🗝 How did Isaiah respond to the revealed holiness of God? What did his words reveal about his heart?

Relatively speaking Isaiah was a good and righteous man. But the majestic light of God's holiness left Isaiah exposed and vulnerable. In his book, *The Holiness of God*, R. C. Sproul describes the experience like this:

> As long as Isaiah could compare himself to other mortals, he was able to sustain a lofty opinion of his own character. The instant he measured himself against the ultimate standard he was destroyed—morally and spiritually annihilated. He was undone. He came apart. His sense of integrity collapsed.

Isaiah recognized his sin in the light of God's holy perfection. God not only revealed Isaiah's sin, He also cleansed it. The coal applied to Isaiah's lips was taken from the altar of sacrifice. On this altar, bulls, goats, and lambs were sacrificed for the people's sin. These offerings represented Jesus Christ, the perfect sacrifice to come, whose death would provide ultimate and eternal forgiveness.

Reread Isaiah 6:8. How did Isaiah respond to God's call for a messenger?

Isaiah was a clean vessel, ready for God's use. After experiencing God's forgiveness and restoration, Isaiah humbly and willingly submitted his life to God's purposes. Then he obediently answered God's call to "go."

🖊 How would you compare your "righteousness" to your co-workers, neighbors, and people you know in the community and society at large? Be honest!

____ They all do a much better job at following God.

____ We're about the same.

____ I live a better, more righteous life than most of them.

🖊 Now, contemplate the holy God of Isaiah's vision. Compare yourself to the exalted Lord. Circle any of the following words that describe your response.

humility	repentance	undone
awe	conviction	worship

Other words to describe your response: _____

_____

_____

God reveals Himself and His holiness to us to call us to repentance and submission. He wants to use us for His purposes. He longs for us to walk closely with Him in humble service. He calls us to be holy as He is holy. Then we can know the intimacy of His presence.

How have the examples of God's revealed holiness impacted you this week? Has it awakened a humble desire to be holy and to draw ever closer to the holy One? Express your thoughts to God below.

Into His Arms! Embracing a Life of Holiness

Life changed dramatically for Janet after her divorce in the late 1970s. As a young, single mom she had to venture out into both the work and social worlds. Unfortunately, instead of clinging to the truth Janet knew from childhood, she conformed to the culture, which taught to "do what feels right to you." Janet spent the next 17 years doing just that. "I didn't think I needed God. I thought I could handle things just fine by myself." In the process, Janet wandered further and further away from God.

After 17 years of wilderness wandering, Janet attended a revival. During the altar call, the pastor asked a question God used to rip off her spiritual blinders. "If you died tonight, are you ready to meet God?" She was not.

Janet caught a glimpse of the holiness of God that night and knew the way she was living her life did not please Him. She knew her disobedience had consequences, but God also reminded her of His forgiveness and grace. He had been waiting for her to return. "God pines for His prodigals to return to Him. He never gives up. That day when I experienced His call to me to return, I sensed Him standing with open arms ready to give me a big hug."

Overwhelmed with repentance and humility, Janet knelt in prayer to give her life back to God. "I told Him this prodigal girl had returned and I would go wherever He led." Within six months Janet had married a godly man, and soon after she entered seminary. Eventually she went into full-time ministry and started the Woman to Woman Mentoring Ministry at Saddleback Church.

Janet frequently tells this story when she speaks to women. She emphasizes that our holy God is a God of redemption and second chances. He never gives up on His children. He is always waiting to trade our ashes for His beauty (Isaiah 61:3).

Has God ever reminded you of His holiness to convict you of a sin in your life?

Have you ever lived in a long-term state of rebellion against God? If so, how did God draw you back to Himself? If not, how can remembering God's holiness foster a life that pleases God?

How can reflecting on God's holiness help us develop greater humility?

As we close this week, spend a few moments thinking about some of the "second chances" God has given you. Praise Him and thank Him for His mercy and grace!

an extreme makeover

wo years ago, our daughter, Kelley, and her husband, Jeremy, bought their first home. They were so excited to be homeowners. The house definitely met their needs, but because it was built in the 1980s, it needed some updating.

They had a month between closing on the house and the end of the lease on their rented duplex. Ahead of time, they made a list of the things they wanted to do, picked out colors, and bought the materials. They closed on the house in the morning, and right after lunch they started work.

Since Jeremy is Mr. Handyman Deluxe, they could do it themselves. The job required just a little money, a lot of time, and even more energy. Thankfully, Kelley and Jeremy didn't have to do it alone. Siblings, friends, and even parents volunteered their time.

Only Jeremy had the expertise to accomplish some of the tasks, such as rounding all the square wall corners, adding stone veneer to the fireplace, building the wooden mantel, and pouring the concrete hearth. Jeremy's brother and father laid hardwood in the guest room. Then the rest of us worked on the "unskilled" jobs, such as smoothing off the "popcorn" ceilings and painting all the walls and trim.

By the time they moved out of the duplex and into the house, the work was complete. The transformation was beautiful. It was worth all the money, time, and energy. Kelley and Jeremy were proud of their new home, and we all celebrated with them.

Fellow believer, before God saved us we were in bad shape—in need of some serious spiritual renovation. But unlike Kelley and Jeremy's house, we didn't have anything to do with this makeover. In fact, we couldn't do anything. It was a work of God from beginning to end.

At the foot of the Cross, Christ took our sin and gave us His holiness. When God saved us, He completely transformed our spirit and declared us

83

"holy" before Him. This *positional* holiness was accomplished for us completely at the will of God through Christ's redeeming work. This week, we will explore our own spiritual "before and after." We will see that believers are *positionally* holy before God because Christ gives us His holiness when He saves us. We will also hear God's call to *progressive* holiness. In this process of sanctification our character and behavior will become increasingly holy and Christlike.

spiritual "before and after"

We've all seen them many times. Those before-and-after photos that portray the dramatic difference some diet, makeover, or remodeling project wrought. Even many popular television shows find their success in the before-and-after theme. The before lacks something vital, suffers from some affliction, or fails to fulfill its purpose. The after has received what it lacked, been healed and made whole, and can meet its fullest potential. We love this transformation, the process of becoming an after.

Ephesians 2 reads like an episode of *Extreme Makeover: Spiritual Edition*. Paul paints a graphic picture of what we looked like before God saved us. Then Paul reveals the beautiful after portrait. He also clearly shows us what Christ did to cause the transformation.

Read straight through Ephesians 2:1–22 to get the big picture.

Now, slowly work your way back through the passage. As you do, in the left side of the table, list all words, phrases, and facts that describe our condition "before" God saved us.

Before Christ	After Christ

This is absolutely the saddest before picture I've ever seen. My list is long and ugly! How about yours?

Before we move to the after, let's wade through all that ugly and take a closer look at two key truths about our lives before Christ: (1) We were dead in our sins. (2) We were separated from God.

Read Romans 5:12 and 6:23. Explain in your own words why we were "dead" and separated from God before He saved us.

Sin brings spiritual death. All of us are sinners. Before God saved us, our spirits were dead because of our sin—unable to commune with God, who is Spirit (John 4:24). We could not reach Him. We were without God and without hope (Ephesians 2:12). We were "deserving of wrath"—deserving of God's punishment (v. 3). But, praise God, He "made us alive with Christ!" (v. 5).

Look through Ephesians 2 once more. This time look for the words and phrases describing our condition after God saved us, and write them in the right column of the table above. When possible write them across from the corresponding condition in the left column. For instance, before salvation we were "dead in our transgression" but after salvation we are "alive in Christ."

I hope you have a little room left in your table. We're going to look at one more passage to bring our before-and-after pictures into sharp focus.

Read Titus 3:3–7. Watch for any additional before-and-after descriptions. Add them to the table above.

According to Titus 3:5, how does God save us? How are our dead spirits born again?

The Apostle John recorded a conversation about spiritual rebirth between Jesus and a Pharisee named Nicodemus. This religious leader, who visited Jesus under the cover of darkness, knew he needed something. And Nicodemus obviously suspected Jesus might have what he was missing.

Read John 3:1–8. Although Nicodemus did not ask Jesus a question, based on Jesus' reply, what questions do you think were on Nicodemus's mind?

Nicodemus risked his reputation and political standing by coming to Jesus for spiritual guidance. Nicodemus was supposed to be the expert in the law. He was supposed to be the one with the answers. Instead, he secretly came to the teacher from Galilee with questions he couldn't even voice. Can't you just picture Nicodemus stammering and looking at the ground? I imagine him then looking up with astonishment when the Rabbi spoke of the very things that were on his heart. *What must I do to be saved?*

Look again at verse 3. What did Jesus say must happen for someone to be saved or "see the kingdom of God"?

According to verse 8, who causes this spiritual rebirth?

In our society, there seems to be an idea that you can be Christian without being one of those radical, fanatical "born-again Christians." But just because some talk show host says it doesn't make it true. This is far from biblical.

Based on the passages we've read today, how would you respond to the idea that you can be a Christian without being born again?

Have you been born again? Has the Holy Spirit given new life to your sin-dead spirit and brought you into a relationship with Jesus Christ? If not, don't go another day without receiving the free gift of salvation God offers.

The need for spiritual rebirth is consistent throughout Scripture. Dead spirits cannot have a relationship with God. We must be born again. The Holy Spirit must do His work. He must completely make us over.

This makeover is so dramatic that I really shouldn't call it a makeover. God didn't just slap some lipstick and mascara on our faces and cover up our gray. He brought the dead to life! Before salvation we were slaves to sin and dead to God. After salvation we are dead to sin and alive to God! (See Romans 6:11.) We didn't just get a makeover, we received a complete change of eternal condition. Hallelujah!

God's salvation not only changes our eternity, it also changes our here and now. Before salvation we lived for ourselves, "gratifying the cravings of our sinful nature" (Ephesians 2:3). But God remade us. We now no longer live for ourselves but for Him and His purposes. God "repurposed" us.

Not long ago, I met with a staff member of a local church. After our meeting she gave me a tour of their lovely facility. The older section of the building had just been remodeled and updated. My guide used the term *repurposed* to highlight the fact that the rooms were being used differently than they had been before. For instance, the former sanctuary is now a gathering room for groups, and old children's classrooms are now offices for preschool staff.

Reread Ephesians 2:10 from the Amplified Bible below:

> *For we are God's [own] handiwork (His workmanship), recreated in Christ Jesus, [born anew] that we may do those good works which God predestined (planned beforehand) for us [taking paths which He prepared ahead of time], that we should walk in them [living the good life which He prearranged and made ready for us to live].*

According to this verse, what is God's purpose for our new life in Christ?

As we close today, think about your own spiritual before and after. If God saved you early in life, your story may not be as physically dramatic, but God performed the same spiritual makeover. Express your gratitude to your Savior in the space below.

the great exchange

Kyle McDonald dreamed of owning a house. He didn't want to spend any money; he wanted to trade for it. So, inspired by the childhood game "Bigger and Better," the 26-year-old Canadian man put his sales job on hold to focus on the trading game.

Kyle started by offering one red paper clip on Craigslist. Soon, two young women who thought the game was fun traded a fish-shaped ink pen for Kyle's paper clip. The pen became a whimsical doorknob, which became a camping stove, which became a generator.

The trading game was off and running, so Kyle started a website. The traded items continued to get bigger and better and included items such as a snowmobile, a recording contract, and an afternoon with Alice Cooper. One year and 14 trades later, Kyle traded a speaking part in a movie with the town of Kipling, Saskatchewan, for a key to his very own house.

Kyle got a house for no money. All it took was 12 months and one red paper clip. That's a pretty good trade. But I know of one trade much "bigger and better." Jesus willingly makes this trade with all who will receive it. Jesus takes our sin and gives us His righteousness.

Yesterday, we closely examined our spiritual before and after. Today, we'll explore how Jesus' work on the Cross makes our after possible. What did our eternal makeover require? We will also recall why we need salvation and how God provides for it. Then we'll discover what we receive in this great exchange.

Read Romans 3:20–26 and 6:23. Based on these passages, for each of the following statements, circle either the T for True or the F for False.

T   F   Every person is a sinner.

T   F   Because of our sin we have earned the death penalty.

T   F   We do not deserve eternal condemnation.

T   F   If we are really good and work really hard, we can be righteous.

T   F   We can only receive righteousness through faith in Christ.

T   F   Jesus' sacrificial death makes our redemption possible.

Without Christ's salvation, we sinners stand eternally condemned (John 3:18). We can do nothing to save ourselves. So, because He loves us, God sent His Son to pay the penalty our sin deserves. The penalty was death. Jesus willingly gave His life to pay our debt.

Read Leviticus 17:11 and Hebrews 9:13–14, 22, 27–28. Why was Jesus' shed blood and death necessary? Mark all that apply.

___ Blood represents life.
___ Atonement or forgiveness requires death/the shedding of blood.
___ The blood of animals can only bring outward cleanliness.
___ Jesus was "unblemished," so His blood can cleanse our consciences.
___ Jesus' sacrifice is completely sufficient for forgiveness and salvation.

Only Jesus' sacrificial death is sufficient to provide our eternal salvation. His life satisfied our death penalty. His shed blood makes our forgiveness possible. His life given for our life. What an incredible exchange! Let's take a closer look at what Jesus traded with us through His sacrifice.

Week 4
Day 2
91

Read the following passages, and use the truths found there to fill in the columns in the table below.

	Jesus Took Our . . .	Jesus Gave Us His . . .
Isaiah 53:5–6		
John 3:16–18		
Romans 4:23–25		
2 Corinthians 5:21		
1 Peter 3:18		

Are you jumping up and down yet? Didn't I tell you this trade was far better than a house? On the Cross, Jesus accomplished for us what we could never do for ourselves.

Have you ever owed a debt someone else paid for you? I've seen it happen to someone else. My friend Sue is a loving person who always looks for ways to help others. Sue once loaned her car to friends while she was out of town. Several weeks later Sue received a speeding ticket in the mail. A photo of her license plate had been taken as her car passed through an intersection. The ticket listed the location and date of the speeding incident.

Sue didn't remember driving down that particular street. Then she noticed the date. She hadn't even been in town. The borrowing friends were driving her car on that day. Sue knew her friends could not afford the ticket as easily as she could. Sue paid the debt and never even told her friends about the ticket.

This small act of grace illustrates what Christ did for us on the Cross. We can't pay the price of salvation. We can't earn it and we don't deserve it. Yet, God gives it to us freely.

Now, I want us to see something else. Jesus' death provided forgiveness for our sins and breached the divide that separated us from God.

Read Romans 5:1–2. How are we able to be at peace with God?

The verb *justify* refers to a judicial act. It is the opposite of condemned. Through faith in Christ, God declares us to be righteous — or holy. God removes our condemnation and places Christ's righteousness on us. God will not hold our sin against us. The penalty has been paid. Christ has taken our sin and God credits our spiritual account with Christ's sacrifice.

Justification is a legal standing and not an internal condition. In his book, *Systematic Theology*, Wayne Grudem emphasizes this fact: "It is important to emphasize that this legal declaration in itself does not change our internal nature or character at all. In this sense of 'justify,' God issues a legal declaration about us."

This legal declaration of righteousness is often referred to as "positional holiness." From a legal standpoint we *are* holy in God's sight because we have Christ's holiness. We have all the blessings and privileges of His holy children. Although salvation provides us with positional holiness, it does not automatically impart holy character and behavior. That comes through the lifelong process of sanctification or "progressive holiness," in which we become increasingly holy and Christlike. Therefore, Christians are both holy and still becoming holy.

Before we end today, let's briefly explore an awesome privilege granted to us as God's "holy" children. Compare Romans 5:1–2 with Ephesians 2:18. What special access do we now have as ones who have been "justified"?

The unholy cannot enter the presence of the holy. But praise God! When Christ took our sin, He gave us His righteousness. We now have legal standing to enter God's holy presence.

Read Hebrews 10:19–23. According to verse 19, in what manner can we enter God's presence?

Week 4
Day 2
93

Based on this passage and what we've studied today, what makes it possible for us to enter God's presence and boldly approach His throne of grace?

Jesus' great exchange makes all this possible — not because we are worthy but because He is worthy! The blood of Jesus has won our entrance into God's presence.

As we close today, draw near to God. Sit before His throne and bask in the glory of His presence.

holiness calling

I know of a church most of us would probably be ashamed to call our church. The body is divided over loyalty to various leaders, with one faction claiming allegiance to one minister and other factions claiming allegiance to others. These divisions foster ongoing quarrels, jealousy, and disagreements.

Members regularly take other members to court over trivial matters. The believers cheat and wrong each other. Then instead of practicing forgiveness or working out their problems with the help of the church, those "wronged" greedily sue their fellow Christians in front of unbelievers.

Sexual immorality runs rampant. In fact, it's worse in this church than it is out in the world. One man even had an affair with his stepmother. Instead of being filled with grief, some in the church boasted over this "freedom."

The members of this church abuse the Lord's Supper. They eat the bread and drink the cup without remembering Christ's sacrifice. They participate with unrepentant hearts and complete disregard for the needs of their fellow Christians.

Individuals with high-profile spiritual gifts feel superior to other members and put them down. They squabble constantly over who has the greater gifts and who is more important. Rather than loving each other and using their gifts to serve God together, they act like children and defame the name of Christ with their unholy behavior.

Do you know of any churches like this? You may have heard of this one. If not, you can read all about it in Paul's first letter to the Christians in Corinth. Sin filled the Corinthian church in the first century. Would you describe it as "holy"? Paul did. But Paul also called them to holiness. Paul's greeting to the church in 1 Corinthians reflects what we discussed yesterday — positional holiness and progressive holiness.

Read 1 Corinthians 1:1–3. In verse 2, how does Paul describe the church in Corinth that seems contradictory to its behavior?

The Greek verb *hagiazo*, or *sanctify* in most English translations, means "to make holy." The verb form is the perfect participle passive. In this passage, the passive verb form refers back to God, denoting He carried out the action toward the Corinthian believers. They had nothing to do with it. "Perfect" expresses completeness. Their holiness—wrought by God through Christ—is an accomplished action, a done deal.

Paul described their positional holiness before God. They had legal standing as God's children. They had been justified by the blood of Christ. They had the privilege to enter God's presence. Yet their lives did not match their legal standing. They were just beginning their journey toward holy behavior and character. They had both been "made holy" and were "called to be holy."

If we read through the entire letter of 1 Corinthians, we would see that Paul essentially said to them: "Your behavior does not matching your calling. Now that you are holy, act like it!" Like the first-century believers in Corinth, God also commands us to live out in our lives the reality of what He has declared us to be. We live in the now and the not yet. The done and the still becoming. The holy and the called to be holy.

Read the following verses and write a brief summary of each.

2 Corinthians 7:1

1 Thessalonians 4:3

1 Timothy 4:7–8

Hebrews 5:14

Hebrews 12:13–14

1 Peter 1:14–16

2 Peter 1:3–4

2 Peter 3:11–14

1 John 3:3

Make a list of words or phrases, found in the passages above, that describe the kind of life God calls us to live. For instance, in 2 Corinthians 7:1, Paul uses the words *purify* and *perfecting holiness.*

Now, using what you've learned in the previous two exercises, write one summary statement describing God's call to progressive holiness.

Every believer is a bit like the Christians in Corinth. Legally we are holy before God. We are indeed saints, clothed with Christ's holiness with our sins forgiven. Yet God calls us to move on from there — to live a life in actuality that reflects our legal standing. To be holy and to live holy.

I don't want to remain forever like the believers Paul wrote about in 1 Corinthians. They had positional holiness before God but did not live holy before God. They accepted the privilege of the relationship with God, but did not reflect His character. This reminds me a little of Prince Harry.

Prince Henry of Wales, the younger son of Prince Charles and Princess Diana, has not been the model royal. A prince by birth, Harry possesses all the privilege, power, and prestige royalty provides. However, Harry often doesn't act in a way that reflects his station in life. Stories abound about drinking, drugs, and Las Vegas carousing.

But there are also stories of courage and character in Harry's military service. It seems he might be growing up and growing into his royal position. Harry is a royal work in progress. And so are we. You and I are princesses, daughters of the King. We are royal works in progress. Holiness doesn't happen overnight; it's a process of leaving the world and its ways behind and adopting the character of Christ.

Do you believe God's call to holiness applies to you? (Circle one.)

Yes   No   Not sure

So far in your Christian walk, how have you responded to His call?

____ Before now, I did not realize God had called me to live a holy life.

____ I knew He called me to holiness, but I ignored the call, delaying my obedience.

____ I knew I should live a holy life, but I didn't know what it should look like.

____ I've been trying to live a holy life, but I have not had much success.

____ I have grown in holiness, but am still growing.

As we continue our study together, we will explore what holiness looks like in our day-to-day lives. We will talk about the difficult and the practical and get down to some nitty-gritty details. But today I want to share this statement by Henry Blackaby from his book, *Holiness*. He describes a believer's pursuit of holiness in a comprehensive way.

> The Scripture says we need to pursue holiness. That is, we need to let the full measure of the nature of God become the pattern for our characters. We need to let Him form in us the full measure of the righteousness of Christ. We need to let

Him take every part of our minds and our hearts and keep them holy unto Himself.

As we close today, spend a moment in prayer. Acknowledge God's call to holiness. Ask Him to help you answer His call. Ask Him to take every part of your mind and heart and make them holy for Him.

power source

I like to think I'm pretty strong and capable—for a middle-aged grandma. I've done a few things a lot of women haven't done. For instance, I've roofed a house, herded cattle, and slept in a tent in the bush of Mozambique.

OK, I'm exaggerating on the herding cattle thing. But I did ride a four-wheeler through a pasture around a bunch of cows. And when I helped roof a house on a missions trip, I did not even attempt to haul the bundle of shingles up the ladder, although another woman with our group did it without a problem!

Like everyone, I have limits and weaknesses, both physically and spiritually. When I was younger, I was much more hesitant to admit to these. I wanted to be able to do it myself, to not ask for help. But as I've "matured," I'm quicker to acknowledge my dependence and need for help.

Yesterday, we studied God's call to holiness. I acknowledge His command and want to obey it. I long to be holy as He is holy. But I can't do it. Not on my own. I do not have the spiritual strength to turn away from sin and embrace holiness. Oh, I can do it some of the time with discipline and sheer will power. But to live a consistent life of holiness, I need help. I must depend fully on God and the power He supplies. Today, we will see how the power of Jesus' resurrection can help us live the holy life that pleases God.

Read 1 Corinthians 15:1–8. List the elements of "first importance" that Paul passed on to the believers in Corinth.

In these few short verses, Paul encapsulates the gospel message: Jesus died for our sins. He was buried. He was raised to life three days later. Jesus death, burial, and resurrection were prophesied throughout the Old Testament. His burial proves His death. And multiple eyewitnesses prove His resurrection.

Read 1 Corinthians 15:17–19. According to these verses, if Christ has not been raised, what would be the result? (Mark all that apply.)
____ Our Christian faith is futile.
____ Our sins have not been forgiven.
____ There is no hope for eternity.
____ We should be pitied for committing our lives to a lie.

Jesus' sacrificial death for our sins is not the complete gospel. The Cross, alone, is not enough. Jesus' death was not sufficient to provide the abundant, victorious life God promises us. Without the Resurrection, Jesus is just another dead prophet. Our hope for this life and the next depends on the resurrection of Jesus from the dead. When He rose from the grave, He proved that everything He said was true.

"But Christ has indeed been raised from the dead" (1 Corinthians 15:20). God has given us "new birth into a living hope through the resurrection of Jesus Christ from the dead" (1 Peter 1:3). Yes, Jesus' death paid the price of our sin, but His resurrection provided our hope for life—both now and eternally. Jesus' victory over death also makes it possible for us to have victory over sin. Let's take a look.

Read Romans 6:1–23. Summarize the main truths of this chapter in a couple of sentences or a few bullet points.

Paul begins this chapter with a question he considered to be ridiculous. "Since God extends His grace to sinners, shouldn't we just go on sinning so He can extend more grace?" (That's my paraphrase.) Paul emphatically insisted this was illogical. Believers should not allow sin to control them because we have "died to sin." He expounds on this truth through the rest of the chapter because this truth is vital for believers' holiness.

Look back at verses 3–5. Describe how a believer identifies with Jesus' death, burial, and resurrection.

In verse 5, Paul says we have been "united with" Christ in both His death and His resurrection. According to *Vine's Complete Expository Dictionary*, the Greek word translated as "united with" in the NIV, means "to make to grow together." It also "indicates the union of the believer with Christ."

This truth goes beyond the symbolic. It is spiritual reality. When Jesus saved us, we died to our old life. We were "raised" to a new life founded solely in Christ. Christ is our life. His resurrection made our new life possible.

Reread verses 6–10. Fill in the following blanks based on the truths found in this passage.
- Because our old selves were crucified with Christ, we are no longer _____ to sin.
- Because we died, we have been _____ from the power of sin.
- Because Jesus was raised from the dead, _____ no longer has power over Him.
- Because Jesus died to sin and lives for God, we must count ourselves dead to _____ and _____ to God.

Jesus' resurrection changed everything. Because He was raised to life, never to die again, He defeated death and broke the hold of sin. Before God saved us, we were slaves to sin. Death was our master. But when we died with Christ, we died to sin. Sin and death no longer have power over us. We are free to live our new lives in Christ. Jesus' victory is our victory! This is a spiritual reality. But we also must choose to walk in it.

Reread Romans 6:11–14. List all the direct commands to believers in these verses. I count at least five.

These commands are the practical application of the truths we discovered earlier in the chapter. Because Jesus broke the power of sin and death, and because we are "united with Him," we can step out in obedience to these commands. The result? Instead of continuing in a habitual pattern of sin (v. 1) our lives will be tools of God's righteousness (v. 13).

Reread Romans 6:19–23 and fill out the table below. List all the results of slavery to sin in the left column and all the results of slavery to God/righteousness in the right column.

Slavery to Sin	Slavery to God

According to verses 19 and 22, what does a life lived as a slave to God lead to?

When we die to our old self and live a new life in Christ as a slave to righteousness, our lives will exhibit ever-increasing holiness. This ever-increasing holiness fosters ever-increasing intimacy with God as we continue to rid our hearts and minds of the sin that prevents us from drawing close to Him.

Sounds great, doesn't it? But is it really possible to consistently say no to sin and yes to righteousness? It's nice to know intellectually that sin has no power over us, but what about power to live that out? Before we close today, let's look at one more glorious truth about the power to live holy lives.

Read 2 Peter 1:3–4. According to verse 3, what has God's divine power given us?

According to verse 4, what will be the benefit when we "participate in the divine nature?"

Now read Ephesians 1:18–20 from the Amplified Bible below:

> *By having the eyes of your heart flooded with light, so that you can know and understand the hope to which He has called you, and how rich is His glorious inheritance in the saints (His set-apart ones), And [so that you can know and understand] what is the immeasurable and unlimited and surpassing greatness of His power in and for us who believe, as demonstrated in the working of His mighty strength, Which He exerted in Christ when He raised Him from the dead and seated Him at His [own] right hand in the heavenly [places].*

Look back at verse 19. List the adjectives Paul uses to describe the power of God in us.

This power God makes available to us — His holy people — also did something else. According to verse 20, what was it?

Believer, the Holy Spirit lives within you and me. He is the source of God's mighty power within us. This is the same power that raised Jesus from the dead! The same power that defeated death and broke the hold of sin. This resurrection power enables us to say no to sin and yes to holiness.

Throughout our next two weeks of study together, we will explore how we can live in this power to embrace holiness and thus embrace the Holy One. But as we close today, I'd like to offer a prayer for you, adapted from Paul's prayer to the Christians in Ephesus from Ephesians 1:17–19.

Glorious Father, please fill up this sweet believer with the presence and power of your Spirit. Help her to know You more fully and help her understand Your calling on her life more completely. Finally, guide her to yield to the unlimited power You provide so she may live a holy life that pleases You. Amen.

reflect and respond

When somebody does something nice for me, I usually want to recipro-cate or pass it on. Generosity and kindness often generate gratitude that expresses itself in action. For instance, I have witnessed random acts of kindness break out in the Starbucks drive-through line. More than once, the stranger in the car ahead of mine paid for my drink. It's really a nice surprise when you reach the window, the barista hands you your drink, and announces it's already paid for. My first response? Surprise, gratitude, and a desire to bless the person behind me in like manner. Of course, my sinful flesh also does two things: First, I wish I had ordered the venti instead of only the grande. And second, I hope the car behind me isn't a 15-passenger van filled with a high school basketball team.

In general, coffee makes me thankful. Free Starbucks coffee makes me want to do something nice for someone else. The kindness moves me to action. But I have been given a far greater gift than this. And if you're in a saving relationship with Jesus, you have too. Unfortunately, we often take God's gift for granted. We fail to respond to His mighty salvation like we should.

In his letter to the believers in Ephesus, Paul beautifully expounded on the abundant, eternal life we have in Christ. Then he clearly taught that this incredible gift should foster gratitude and motivate us to holiness. Let's take a look.

Read Ephesians 1:3–14.

The verses you just read are all one long sentence in the Greek. Once Paul started praising God, he didn't stop to take a breath for 12 verses! It reminds me of an excited young child who wants so much to tell you everything; she doesn't even slow down enough to breathe. I can see Paul, hunched over the papyrus, writing with excitement and joy over what God has done.

Look back at verse 3. With what has God blessed us?

Compare Ephesians 1:3 with 2 Peter 1:3, a verse we read yesterday. Using the information in this verse from 2 Peter, describe God's purpose for the spiritual blessings and divine power God pours into our lives?

God has not promised us physical health or worldly wealth. His promises are spiritual in nature and eternal in scope. The blessings He lavishes on us are exactly what we need to deepen our relationship with God, grow to Christlikeness, and fulfill God's purposes for our lives.

Contemplating this glorious truth in Ephesians 1, moved Paul to praise. Paul's praise includes a long list (though not exhaustive) of some of the many ways God has indeed "blessed us in the heavenly realms," centering on what the Father has done for us in Christ.

Work your way back through Ephesians 1:4–14. Make a list of all the blessings we have "in Christ."

Look back at your list. This is why Paul got so excited. Don't you just want to shout out loud? Or jump up and down?! We are chosen, adopted, redeemed, and forgiven! God has lavished His grace on us (love this!) and sealed us with the Holy Spirit until we receive our eternal inheritance as His beloved daughters! Amen and amen!

Verses 4–14 are a beautiful description of what God does when He saves us. Before salvation, we are separated from God because of our sin. But then God intervenes! Our salvation is based solely on the character and action of God. The Father initiates our salvation. He chooses us in love and calls us to hope in Christ. Jesus makes our salvation possible by satisfying the requirements that God's justice demands. "The wages of sin is death" (Romans 6:23). Jesus paid our debt with His own blood. The Holy Spirit applies God's saving work. He restores our spiritual life. The Spirit's presence with every believer is God's promise that we belong to Him. The Spirit protects us and guarantees our eternal life to come!

🗝 We've seen what God has blessed us with and how we receive His blessings. Now let's consider *why*. Make a list below of all the reasons you can find in Ephesians 1:3–14.

You may have really had to dig to answer that last question because there are so many treasures hidden in the passage. So, to summarize, God saved us and lavished His blessings on us because:

- He wants to make us holy and blameless (v. 4).
- It pleased Him and He wanted to (v. 5).
- Our salvation will bring Him praise (v. 6).
- He is loving and full of grace (vv. 6–7).
- To carry out His plans and purposes in Christ (vv. 9–11).

🗝 Now read Ephesians 4:1. How should we respond to God's lavish grace and rich blessings? Fill in the blanks.

Live a life _____ of the _____ you have received.

This verse marks a shift in the book of Ephesians. The first three chapters eloquently describe the salvation we have in Christ. This salvation is the "calling" (or "vocation" in the King James Version) Paul refers to here in Ephesians 4:1. Our "calling" is an invitation from God to partake of the divine blessings of redemption. These glorious, eternal blessings deserve a response.

Paul's encouragement to "live a life worthy" of our calling is not merely a suggestion or recommendation. The Greek word translated as "urge" is a serious appeal. Paul pleads with the Ephesians—and with us—to live the kind of life that adequately reflects what God has done for us. Since God has saved us from eternal destruction our lives should reflect our gratitude.

In the second half of his letter, Paul goes into great detail about what grateful, redeemed lives should look like. Next week, we will take a closer look, but as we end this week's study, let's consider a small passage that sums up what our response should be.

Read Ephesians 4:20–24, and fill in the blanks below.
Put off your _____ self, which is being corrupted by sin.
Put on the _____ self, created to be like God.

According to Ephesians 4:24, what characteristics should describe a redeemed life?

God holds nothing back from us, His children. He has blessed us with every spiritual blessing in Christ. He gives us everything we need to live a life of holiness. Let's live a life worthy of this great calling.

As we close today, prayerfully reflect on your blessings from God, which Paul describes in Ephesians 1:3–14. In light of what God has done for you, will you commit to "live a life worthy of your calling?" (4:1).

Into His Arms! Embracing a Life of Holiness

Stephanie's before Jesus story is a particularly difficult one. For nine years of her childhood, she suffered sexual abuse from two extended family members. These painful experiences skewed her concept of love and shaped her teen and early adult years. A series of wrong choices took her further and further away from God.

Pregnant at 17, Stephanie and the father of her baby married, but by 19 she was a single mom. Desperate for love, she hit the bar scene and fell for a drummer in a band. They married, but their life together was not what God intended. Their marriage revolved around rock and roll, bars, and the next gig.

Although Stephanie was needy, she didn't realize it was God she needed until He lovingly intercepted her. She heard the gospel message for the first time from a television evangelist. Then over the course of two years, God continued to draw her to Himself. Finally, in God's time, Stephanie entered into a love relationship with Jesus.

The change in her life was dramatic. Stephanie describes her life before Christ as darkness and her life after Christ as light. "I was one person one minute and then completely different the next. My life took a 180-degree turn. I didn't understand it then, but now I know God dramatically changed my identity in a moment of time."

Immediately hungry to know more about the God who saved her, Stephanie began to read and study the Bible. She learned more about what God had done in her life. Overwhelmed with God's love and the depth of Christ's forgiveness, she longed to be who God created her to be.

I wanted to love Jesus and live for Him. I didn't want to get over that. When the Holy Spirit convicted me of sin, I recognized it grieved God and I didn't want to sin anymore. I longed to be holy because God called me to be holy and gives me the power to be holy. I don't want to spend my life making excuses; I'd rather live in the freedom that comes with holiness. There is such joy living the holy life God called us to live, full of the Spirit and feeling God in every moment. I want my life to be one big thank-You card to Jesus.

Briefly describe your own spiritual before.

How did God get your attention and draw you to Himself?

What difference did His great salvation make in your life?

Your physical before and after may not have been as dramatic as Stephanie's, but the change in your eternal condition was definitely like "darkness and light." Describe the spiritual difference your salvation has made.

Write a thank-you note to God for His great salvation.

light us up!

*O*When I became a mother for the first time at the age of 25, I was completely clueless about taking care of a baby. High school activities had taken priority over teenage babysitting. My beautiful daughter, Kelley, was the first baby I really ever had anything to do with. Diaper changing, feeding, burping, and bathing were all new territory. My husband had less experience than I did.

By God's mercy, my sweet mother stayed with us two weeks to help. She gave me a crash course in mothering and even taught Wayne a thing or two. But the day she left I stood on the porch holding Kelley, sobbing, and thinking, *What am I going to do now?* (In case you're wondering, Kelley did survive. She is a happy, healthy young wife and mother.)

When Kelley was born, I fully became a mother. You can't be "sort of" a mother or halfway a mother. However, I had a lot to learn about how to act like a mother, how to fulfill that role. Three children and more than 25 years later, I've had lots of practice and lots of opportunities to make mistakes. Without a doubt I am a better mother now than I was that day I stood crying on my front porch. But I'm not perfect. I'm still learning how to be a mother.

My sanctification—spiritual growth—is the same. The first time I came to the Cross of Christ many years ago, God the Father declared me to be holy. He exchanged my sin for Christ's righteousness. From that moment on, I stand positionally holy before the throne of God. However, my character, attitudes, and actions are still far from the transcendent holiness of God. Thus began a lifetime of progressive holiness, or sanctification, as God continually shapes me to be more and more like Jesus.

Over the years, God has refined me and worked on my character. I am more like Christ today than I was two decades, or even a month, ago. And even though I still have a long way to go, I continue to push ahead pursuing God's call to holiness. And as I work toward holiness, my holy God draws me ever closer.

it sure is dark in here

Have you taken a good look around lately? The values and behavior of the culture in which we live don't come close to the standards God established for us in His Word. In fact, it looks pretty dark out there. I had hoped I was only imagining that the level of morality in the United States keeps getting worse—then I read some facts that confirmed my observations.

A nationwide survey by the Barna Group contrasted the moral convictions of Americans in their 20s and 30s (the buster generation) with Americans over 40 (referred to as pre-busters). The 32 factors examined cover perspectives and behaviors relating to areas such as sexuality, substance use and abuse, gambling, profanity, and the treatment of others. The busters were "less moral" than the pre-busters in 25 out of the 32 areas. In the remaining seven, they were about the same.

Busters were twice as likely as pre-busters to lie, steal, and actively seek revenge against someone who has offended them. Busters were "significantly more likely to accept gambling, profanity, intoxication, and illegal drug use as morally acceptable behaviors." But the biggest area of change is "Americans' perspectives and behaviors related to sexuality." The majority of Busters (much more than pre-busters), view cohabitation, sex outside of marriage, and viewing pornography as morally acceptable. And while only 25 percent of pre-busters believe homosexuality is acceptable, almost half of busters believe it is.

While this information is startling, the survey uncovered one more fact that should cause Christians everywhere to grieve. Statistics showed only slight distinction between busters in general and born-again busters. In fact, they were virtually identical in half of the factors tested. "Born again Busters were much less likely to act in a 'moral' manner than born again adults over forty." In regard to the attitudes of born-again busters, the director of the research, David Kinnaman, pointed out, "The research shows that people's moral profile is more likely to resemble that of their peer group than it is to take shape around the tenets of a person's faith."

Overall, the younger generation of Christians today is being shaped more by the world than by Christ. If this continues, soon the church will look just like the world! There has never been a greater need for holiness. God commands His people to be a light in the darkness. And it is certainly dark out there. We must shine the light of God's holiness into the darkness.

Read Ephesians 4:17–24. Does God call believers to be like the world or like Himself?

In this part of his letter to the Christians in Ephesus, Paul contrasts the lives of the Gentiles (those who do not belong to God) with those who know Christ (Christians). He "insists" that the believers must no longer live like the unbelievers.

Check all the phrases below that Paul uses to describe the unbelieving Gentiles (See Ephesians 4:17–19).

___ Futile thinking   ___ No sensitivity to sin

___ Darkened understanding   ___ Given over to sensuality

___ Separated from the life of God   ___ Indulges in all kinds of impurity

___ Ignorant   ___ Continual lust for more

___ Hard hearts

Does this sound anything like our world today? (Circle one.)

Yes   No   Somewhat

Although the media glamorizes our self-absorbed, anything-goes culture, the consequences of this kind of lifestyle are, sadly, all around us. Our jails and rehab centers are bursting at the seams. The teen pregnancy rate in the United States is higher than most other industrialized countries. Every year, the deaths of 5,000 young people can be directly contributed to underage drinking.

This is just a sampling of the heartache and bondage that sin brings. While many believers may not struggle with these particulars issues, other more "acceptable" sins, such as materialism, pride, and gossip, still bring consequences, including distance in our relationship with God.

Fill in the blanks in the statements below to complete Paul's instructions to the believers about no longer living "as the Gentiles do." We did a similar

exercise last week, but this is a truth we need to reinforce again and again.
(See Ephesians 4:20–24.)

- In regard to your former way of life, _____ _____
  your old self and its deceitful _____ .
- Be made _____ in the _____ of your minds.
- Put on the _____ self, created to be like God in true righteousness and _____ .

Paul emphasized transformation in this passage. When we came to know Christ, God freed us from bondage to the dark futility of this world. We must no longer conform to the image of that world. We must take off the old self and put on the new. God did not create us to be like the world. He created us to be holy like He is holy.

How is the church doing with transformation today? In what ways do you see that the church still looks very much like the world? How can you help lead the way toward transformation?

Week 5
Day 1
112

Read Romans 12:1–2:

> *Therefore, I urge you, brothers, in view of God's mercy, to offer your bodies as living sacrifices, holy and pleasing to God — this is your spiritual act of worship. Do not conform any longer to the pattern of the world, but be transformed by the renewing of your mind. Then you will be able to test and approve what God's will is — his good, pleasing, and perfect will.*

"Therefore" refers to Paul's beautiful exposition of our salvation in Christ in the first 11 chapters of the Book of Romans. Given God's mercy in saving us, we should respond with nothing less than our whole selves. Verse two elaborates on how our lives can be a living sacrifice — holy and pleasing to God. We are not to be conformed to the world but transformed into something else entirely. Something that is pleasing to God. Holy. Transformed from the world's mold and conformed to the image of God's holy nature.

In your current spiritual condition, do you look more like the world or like Christ? Let's be honest with ourselves and with God.

If you long to be truly transformed, end today by rewriting Romans 12:1–2 in your own words as a prayer to God.

day two

somebody turn on a light

The thunderstorms common in our region of Texas cause frequent power outages. We stay stocked up on flashlight batteries and lantern fuel, but sometimes a loss of electricity takes us by surprise and if those items aren't handy, we're left groping around in the dark.

That's why I was so excited about one particular stocking stuffer I found last Christmas. This unusual item looks like your average nightlight, but works differently. Plugged into an outlet in our bedroom, it only lights up when the power supply is cut off. If we lose electricity in the middle of the night, the light shines bright enough for us to find our way to a flashlight. Brilliant!

God desires His children to be like that backward nightlight. When everything around us is dark, we should be a light pointing the way to Christ. That's what a holy life does. It stands out like a light in our dark culture. But what does a holy life look like in daily life? Today's lesson will help us build a good picture by considering three passages that contrast an unholy life with a holy life.

🔑 Read the following passages, and use the information you find to complete the table below. List unholy behaviors and attitudes on the left and holy behaviors and attitudes on the right. Take your time, and ask God to show you what He wants you to learn about holiness from these passages. Keep in mind that a behavior or attitude may be implied.

Galatians 5:16–25

Ephesians 4:25 to 5:7

Colossians 3:1–17

Conformed to the World/Unholy Life	Transformed/Holy Life

Our holy God does not change (Malachi 3:6). He does not change like shifting shadows (James 1:17). He is the same yesterday, today, and forever (Hebrews 13:8). How does this truth apply to the table you completed above?

God's holy nature is transcendently perfect. It never changes. There is no need. Perfection does not change with the times. God's expectations for His children are the same today as they were 2,000 years ago. While cultural mores and socially acceptable behavior change constantly, God does not.

List behaviors and attitudes that our culture considers normal and morally acceptable but fall short of God's unchanging standards. (I've listed a couple to get you started.)
• Living together before marriage.
• Using coarse language and profanity.
• Other:

Yesterday we emphasized that holiness is about transformation—putting off the old self in its likeness to the world and putting on the new self in its likeness to God. I want to emphasize an important truth. Even though we have looked today at specific behaviors and attitudes to help us understand what a holy life looks like, these things are only the outward manifestation of our inward condition. True holiness is not adherence to a long list of do's and don'ts. That's legalism. Without real transformation, we can only keep that up for so long.

Reread Galatians 5:16–18. According to these verses, how do we keep from gratifying our sinful desires and live a life pleasing to God? What does this look like in your everyday life?

As we close today, consider these words by Nancy Leigh DeMoss about conforming to God's holiness:

> Yes, holiness involves adherence to a standard, but the obedience God asks of us is not cold, rigid, and dutiful. It is a warm, joyous, loving response to the God who loves us and created us to enjoy intimate fellowship with Him. It is the overflow of a heart that is deeply grateful to have been redeemed by God from sin. It is not something we manufacture by sheer grit, determination, and willpower. It is motivated and enabled by the Holy Spirit who lives within to make us holy.

Week 5
Day 2
115

step into the light

I love to read. While I do read a lot of nonfiction, one of my favorite pastimes is to curl up with a great story, particularly a good mystery. This passion began in childhood. I spent many hours sitting in the beanbag chair in my bedroom reading Nancy Drew mysteries from cover to cover. (Yeah, I know I just dated myself.) Unfortunately, my choice of reading material has not always been as benign as what new puzzle Nancy and her friends had to solve.

A few years ago, I began to read a popular detective series. I did notice the characters in the book used language I would never hear at church. And their moral standards weren't very high. But the plots intrigued me; I had to keep reading to find out "who dun it." And of course, one book in the series led to another and then another. Although the books had no "outward" effect on me, I did begin to notice a difference in my word choice when I talked to myself.

About that time, I started to listen to God's gentle prodding through the conviction of the Holy Spirit. His direction was clear: "Get rid of those books, and don't read any more like them." This time I obeyed immediately. I say "this time" because I don't always obey immediately. At times I struggle with obedience. Sometimes I have even acknowledged sin, turned away from the behavior or attitude for a while, only to pick it up again later. Does this mean I am unholy? Sometimes my life resembles the unholy side of the table we completed yesterday. But I am a child of God, chosen to be holy before the creation of the world. I stand before God, holy in Christ, yet continuing to perfect holiness out of reverence for God.

Read 2 Corinthians 7:1. What does Paul encourage the Corinthian Christians to do in order to move toward holiness?

✎ Read 2 Corinthians 6:16–18. Check all the statements below that are promises of God for His people who "purify ourselves from everything that contaminates" (7:1).

____ God will live with them, walk among them, and be their God.

____ God will receive them.

____ He will be a Father to them, and they will be His sons and daughters.

Those books contaminated my thought life and compromised my relationship with God. In order to have a pure heart and mind, I had to get rid of them. Yesterday, we explored Scripture to create a word picture. We compared unholy behaviors and attitudes with holy ones. We also considered the truth that holiness is not legalism. We cannot be holy by adhering to a long list of rights and wrongs. If we did we would be no better than the Pharisees that Jesus condemned. However, these behaviors and attitudes do reflect our heart condition before God. In fact, God inspired the Scripture we read yesterday so we could use it as a light to guide our lives. That's exactly what we're going to do today.

Look back at 2 Corinthians 7:1. Paul tells the Corinthian Christians to "purify" or "cleanse" themselves from everything that contaminates. The word in the original Greek language means to "purify from the pollution and guilt of sin." Paul knew that all sin has consequences. Some of the consequences are physical, some are emotional, but all are spiritual. Sin offends our holy God and contaminates our relationship with Him. Those who purify their lives and grow in holiness will enjoy a deeper intimacy with God.

What motivation for holiness does Paul cite in 2 Corinthians 7:1?

We are motivated toward holiness when we "revere" or "fear" God. In Week 1, Day 2, we learned that God expects us to be holy because He is holy. Our holiness is based on the nature of God. The more we understand, recognize, and experience His holiness, the more we will fear or revere Him. Therefore, we can foster holiness in our lives by exploring His holiness.

We are going to spend the rest of today examining our own lives. In what ways do we act like the world? In what ways do we think like the world? Our goal is to allow God to examine our hearts and minds against

His standard. Please hear me: The purpose of this self-evaluation is not to discourage or overwhelm us with how far we have to go. The purpose is to begin our journey toward holiness. God has chosen us and made us holy in Christ. Let's allow Him to continue His work in us.

First, pause and ask God to examine your life and show you specific things that need attention. Now, review the chart we completed yesterday, keeping in mind that God may bring something to your mind that is not on the chart.
- Are there areas that don't meet God's standards?
- Are there areas that are not holy?
- Ask God to bring specific activities, attitudes, and relationships to mind. Don't hurry; take as much time as necessary.
- List whatever He says to you below.

How will you respond to what God has said? There may be activities and behaviors you need to cut out of your life. There may be thought patterns and attitudes you need to allow God to transform. Remember, these things bring consequences whether we see it or not. They are like bricks in a wall that separate us from God. But obedience tears down the wall and opens the way to God's waiting arms.

As we end today, write how you will specifically respond to God. This is your commitment to obedience. When you finish, sign it and date it. Look back at this commitment as often as necessary.

Have you ever started a worthwhile project you failed to finish because the cost was too great? You still wanted the finished product and the benefits you would enjoy, but you weren't willing to give up the time, money, resources, or energy it required. A higher education, a home renovation, and the next great novel are all examples. Sometimes we quit halfway through because we didn't count the cost before we started.

Have you considered the cost of holiness? In his book, *Holiness*, J. C. Ryle, the Victorian era minister and theologian, discusses the cost of being a "real Christian" instead of a "mere outward Christian."

> But it does cost something to be a real Christian, according to the standard of the Bible. There are enemies to be overcome, battles to be fought, sacrifices to be made, an Egypt to be forsaken, a wilderness to be passed through, a cross to be carried, a race to be run. Conversion is not putting a man in an armchair and taking him easily to heaven. It is the beginning of a mighty "counting the cost."

A sober determination of the "cost" of holiness will foster an intimate dependence on God and help us stand firm when trials come. Ryle names four "costs" we should consider:

- First, to pursue holiness we must deny the *self-righteousness* that comes from pride and the misconception of our own goodness.
- Second, we must give up *our sins*. We often love those things that keep us bound.
- Third, holiness will cost us a *life of ease*. To be holy, we must stay on guard, practice discipline, and carefully watch our behavior and attitudes.
- Fourth we will lose *the favor of the world*.

✎ Let's take a closer look at the fourth idea in this list. Read 2 Timothy 3:10–12. After describing the difficulties he himself had endured, what did Paul say would happen to anyone who lives a godly life?

Paul suffered persecutions of many kinds because of his faithful obedience to Jesus Christ. He even made a list that includes imprisonment, floggings, beatings, shipwrecks, bandits, sleeplessness, hunger, thirst, and danger from Jews and Gentiles (2 Corinthians 11:23–28). Paul also said the "Lord rescued me from all of them" (2 Timothy 3:11). Obviously, Paul did not mean that God kept him from experiencing any suffering and persecution. Instead, Paul acknowledged that God was in the midst of his troubles and gave him the strength to get through them.

Paul also recognized the benefits and blessings of suffering. He knew that when believers endure persecution God is glorified. His strength working in our bodies, these "jars of clay," reveals His mighty power to the world (2 Corinthians 4:7–9). Paul knew that when believers are persecuted, as a direct result of obedience to God, they come to know Christ in an experiential way that is only possible through "participation in His sufferings (Philippians 3:10)." Holiness may bring suffering, but it also forges a unique bond with our heavenly Father.

Paul's experience with persecution is not unique. Jesus Himself warned His disciples to expect suffering and persecution because they followed Him. Keep in mind, any and every trial we face is not persecution for the sake of Christ. Some difficulties are the result of our fallen world that everyone experiences. Others are the consequences of our own sin. We only share in the sufferings of Christ when we are persecuted as a direct result of following Christ (1 Peter 4:14–15). Be prepared! Those who seek to live a holy life will be persecuted (2 Timothy 3:12).

✎ Read John 15:18–21. Why does the world persecute believers?

✎ Read John 7:7. Why did the world hate Jesus? (Read the first six verses for the context of the passage. When Jesus said, "The world can't hate you," He was not referring to His disciples but to his half brothers who did not believe in Him.)

Has the world ever "hated" you because of Christ? (Circle one.)

Yes   No

🌱 If not, why do you think you have never experienced any suffering for the sake of Christ?

🌱 Remember J. C. Ryle's four costs are self-righteousness, sins, life of ease, and favor of the world. List some things a life of holiness might cost you. (I have listed a few things just to get you thinking in the right direction. Be as specific to your own life as possible.)
- Job promotion
- A current relationship
- Your favorite television show

Even though an obedient life of holiness will result in some degree of persecution, God will work in it to bring about good. Any and everything we give up, yield, suffer, lose, or endure is nothing compared to the "surpassing worth of knowing Christ" (Philippians 3:8)." Plus, holy living reaps other blessings as well.

🗝 Read the Scripture passages listed below on the left. Draw a line from each passage to the corresponding blessing of holiness listed on the right.

Psalm 15:1–5   Powerful and effective prayer life

Psalm 66:18–20   Life will be a testimony to the lost and bring glory to God

Matthew 5:6   Useful to God and equipped for effective service to Him

Matthew 5:8   Experience joy by remaining in God's love

John 15:10–11   Will see God

2 Timothy 2:21   Will have contentment in God

James 5:16b	Will stand firm and live in God's presence
1 Peter 2:12	Fellowship with God and other believers
1 John 1:3–7	God hears their prayers

Picture with me the life of a believer who truly pursues holiness. Her relationship with God is deep and satisfying. When she prays, God moves. God works in and through her life to accomplish His purposes. She stands strong in her faith and has a constant awareness of God's presence. As she seeks the things of righteousness, her life causes the lost to acknowledge God and give Him glory. Yes, there will be persecutions and sufferings. Whether small or great, the holy believer enjoys an intimate knowledge of Christ she would not have otherwise known. I want to be this believer. Do you?

lifelong lightening

Everything seems to be "instant"—or at least "fast"—in the United States. I'm a firm believer in instant pudding and instant oatmeal. Who wants to go to all the trouble of cooking it when all you have to do is add and stir? And biscuits in a can and cookie dough in a tub are a busy woman's best friends—in more ways than one. I also love my laptop and Internet access. In the space of about three and a half minutes, I can add a thought to an article, check my email, buy a book, and play a game of FreeCell.

Unfortunately, these conveniences and our fast-paced society have conditioned us to expect instant gratification in almost every area of our lives. We don't know how to wait or work for things. If we don't see quick progress in an endeavor we often give up. How does this apply to holiness? We may want holiness, but we want it now!

Next week we will explore how we can begin to live holy lives by cooperating with the indwelling Holy Spirit. But today, I want us to take in one thing: holiness takes a lifetime and beyond. There is no quick fix to sin or fast track to holiness. Larry Page and Sergey Brin, those two Stanford students who started Google, may have become billionaires virtually overnight, but holiness takes time and effort.

Read 2 Corinthians 3:16–18 (NLT) below:

> But whenever someone turns to the Lord, the veil is taken away. Now the Lord is the Spirit, and wherever the Spirit of the Lord is, there is freedom. So all of us who have had that veil removed can see and reflect the glory of the Lord. And the Lord—who is the Spirit—makes us more and more like him as we are changed into his glorious image.

Circle the word *Spirit* in the passage above. What does He do in the believer's life?

The Spirit of God is intimately involved in our spiritual growth. He indwells every believer, freeing us from the burden of sin (Romans 8:1), and then continually works to make us more like Jesus. Remember that holiness is conformity to the nature of God and God's glory is His holiness revealed. So, according to this passage, the Holy Spirit works in us so we will reflect the holiness of God.

Underline the phrase in the 2 Corinthians passage above that describes the progressive and ongoing nature of our holiness. Does this sound like a quick process or something more gradual?

Read 1 Timothy 4:7–8. (Note that *godly* and *godliness* can also be translated as "holy" or "holiness.")

Week 5
Day 5
124

What does Paul say we must do to be godly?

What physical images does this bring to mind? What do you think Paul's metaphor means for our spiritual growth?

I used to run some in my younger days. One fall, a few friends and I trained together for a 10K race. We faithfully met several times a week and stuck to our program. Race day arrived. We all ran, and we all finished. One of those friends continued to train and went on to run a marathon. It took consistent training, commitment, and physical discipline. (Side note: I have not run a marathon.)

Paul was familiar with the Greek games. He knew the physical training and discipline it took to be an athletic champion. He presents this physical picture to represent our spiritual growth and development. The pursuit of holiness is like a marathon. I could not decide today to run a marathon and go out and do it tomorrow. It requires months—or longer—to prepare for that kind of physical trial. We cannot decide today we want to journey toward holiness and be perfectly holy tomorrow. As we obediently cooperate with the Holy Spirit we will make progress, one small victory at a time. From glory to glory as the holiness of Christ shines in our lives more and more.

Are you ready to commit to this lifelong process? Write your commitment to God below.

Into His Arms! Embracing a Life of Holiness

Andy and Linda gave their lives to Christ as a young married couple. A nurturing church welcomed them and their spiritual journey began. Now, more than a decade later, they've built a strong Christian home for their two teenagers. They are leaders in the church and vocal about their faith.

Andy works for a major oil service company in middle management. Recently, he had the responsibility of organizing a social night for employees and customers. The setting of the social night was chosen for him—a local summer theater production with a reputation of being risqué. Andy and Linda both felt uneasy about attending, much less inviting others to go. But did they have a choice?

As the date for the event drew closer, Andy and Linda heard even more bad reports about the production. Linda hoped something would happen that would keep her from attending. "I wanted God to take care of it so I wouldn't actually have to do anything or take a stand."

Andy knew it would not be good for his career to say no to his superiors, so he failed to even express his concerns. He was going and wanted Linda to go. She sensed God telling her no, but Linda agreed to attend. The play turned out to be everything they'd been told. The language was terrible, and the sexual innuendo was worse. Not only were Linda and Andy uncomfortable, so were others at their table. Linda and Andy both regretted not obeying God's clear direction. On a positive note, they both repented and allowed God to teach them something new about obedience.

Have you ever had a similar experience? If so, describe it.

What justifications did you give for disobeying God?

What were the consequences of your disobedience?

Did you wish you had acted differently? If so, how?

Did the experience change how you respond to God?

running into His arms

enny's family doctor is a kind, Christian man. He treated both Jenny and her husband for years. When she needed physical therapy, Jenny was in his office often and they developed a friendship. They regularly chatted about their families and activities. They discussed books and Bible study. He asked about Jenny's husband and their travels. She asked the doctor about his family.

Later in her therapy, Jenny noticed the doctor seemed emotionally down and discouraged, but didn't ask him about it. Then not long after, the doctor told Jenny that he and his wife were struggling in their relationship. Because of their friendship, he felt free to share his feelings with her, but that kind of emotional intimacy made Jenny uncomfortable. She told the doctor that she and her husband would pray for them and then quickly ended the visit.

Jenny believed the doctor was a godly man, but she also knew it would be foolish to offer him her shoulder to cry on. She chose to protect the doctor and herself. The doctor's marital stress made him vulnerable to temptation, and Jenny did not want to foster that in any way—no matter how innocently—or get caught up in temptation herself.

To further guard herself, Jenny made appointments with another physician for a while. And when she and the doctor did meet again, she proceeded very cautiously in their conversation. Thankfully, the doctor and his wife sought counseling and strengthened their marriage.

Even though Jenny's marriage was strong and fulfilling, the Holy Spirit waved a warning flag in her heart. "To offer myself as a confidant to another man was to step off God's path of wisdom. Simply sitting down beside a male friend, responding with a misleading tone, or giving an embrace of support could derail our lives from God's glory. I was not the right one to offer consolation. To do so would have naively compromised my commitment to holiness."

Jenny listened to the Holy Spirit's warning and chose to purposefully chase after holiness. She could have easily ignored the Spirit's prompting, but the results could have been disastrous. The Holy Spirit indwells every believer. He not only warns us of sin and potential spiritual danger, He also gives us the guidance we need to protect ourselves, and the power we need to obey.

In our final week of study together, we will explore how to practically embrace holiness in our daily lives. Holiness will break down barriers that sin erects between ourselves and God, and pave the way for intimacy in our relationship.

training partner

Olympic champion Missy Franklin was born to swim. Her profile on the Olympic website describes her as "built for success." Missy is six feet one and wears size 13 shoes. Her dad jokes that his daughter has "built-in flippers." Add in her six-feet-four-inch arm span, and it's no wonder she's a swimming machine.

In the 2012 summer Olympics in London, Missy won four gold medals and a bronze. She also broke two world records in the London games. First, Missy became the fastest woman ever in the 100-meter backstroke. Second, Missy helped her medley relay team set the record in the 4x100-meter race.

Missy is young enough to take part in possibly three more Olympic games. With time and talent on her side, she has the potential to become the most decorated female Olympic swimmer of all time. Move over, Michael Phelps!

Although Missy is physically equipped for swimming, she could never achieve this kind of success without rigorous training. Missy began her swim training when she was just 7 years old. Now at the age of 18, she trains eight times a week during the school year and nine during the summer months. She swims more than 6,000 yards in a two-hour water workout. In addition, she also does land workouts to build core strength and improve swimming movements. And she does it all at an altitude of 6,000 feet in her home state of Colorado.

Missy's physical traits and dedicated training combined make her an Olympic champion. Without the disciplined workouts, her size and inherent strength alone would not be enough. Likewise, no matter how great her commitment to training, if Missy was not built for swimming her success would be limited. Missy needs both the physical characteristics and talent God gave her, plus the intense purposeful training. This combination of physical power and disciplined effort creates a highly successful partnership.

A believer's pursuit of holiness is also a partnership. We cannot do it without the power of the indwelling Holy Spirit. And He demands our obedient, intentional cooperation. In today's lesson, we'll see how God designed this partnership.

Read 2 Peter 1:3–4. (We read this passage in Week 4, but today we're going to dig a little deeper.) What does God supply so we can live a godly life and escape the corruption of the world?

Yes, God calls His children to holiness. But He also gives us the power we need to obey. "His divine power has given us everything we need for life and godliness!" *The Complete Word Study New Testament* defines "godliness" as "devotion, piety, and worship toward God; a general sense of a pious life or a life which is morally good." To live a godly life is to live the holy life that reflects God's nature and pleases Him.

Week 6
Day 1
130

In Week 4, we learned how we receive this divine power. But to emphasize this important truth, let's hear it again from Jesus' mouth.

Read Acts 1:8. According to Jesus, how would His disciples get the power they needed to carry out His Great Commission?

The Greek word translated as "power" in both 2 Peter 1:3 and Acts 1:8 is *dunamis*. It can refer to might, ability, power, or miraculous works. In fact, the power can even be quite "explosive," thus our English derivative "dynamite." *Dunamis* is used to describe a variety of divine activity in the New Testament, including Jesus' miracles. Let's take a quick look at some of these other passages.

Read the following passages and beside each describe what God's power working in us can accomplish. (Note: Beside each passage, I've listed the verse or verses that contain the Greek word *dunamis*.)

Acts 19:11 (v. 11)

1 Corinthians 2:4–5 (vv. 4, 5)

Ephesians 3:16–20 (vv. 16, 20)

Colossians 1:10–11 (v. 11)

Colossians 1:28–29 (v. 29)

2 Timothy 1:7–8 (vv. 7, 8)

These examples of the working of God's power in the lives of believers are just a sample. Our God is "able to do immeasurably more than all we ask or imagine, according to His power (*dunamis*) that is at work within us." That should blow our socks off!

Of course we really like to quote this verse (Ephesians 3:20) when we want to do some great deed for God or when we have a trial or difficulty in our life we can't seem to overcome. But what about living a life of holiness? This same "immeasurably more" power is available to us as we seek to live a holy life that pleases God. Great, right? So we can just sit back and let God make us holy? Not quite.

Week 6
Day 1
131

Go back to 2 Peter 1:5–9. Peter begins this passage, "For this very reason," pointing readers back to something he's just written. To what "reason" is Peter referring?

Because God has given us power to live a godly life, we are to "make every effort" to live a godly and Christlike life. The Greek noun translated as "effort" in the NIV or "diligence" in the King James is *spoud* . *Vine's Complete Expository Dictionary of Old and New Testament Words* defines *spoud* as "earnestness, zeal, or carefulness."

In addition to "knowledge" and six Christlike character traits, what does Peter also say we should "make every effort" to add to our faith? (Look at v. 7.)

According to verse 8, why would we want to make the effort to add these things?

Let's put this together. Peter said God's divine power has given us every-thing we need for godliness (2 Peter 1:3). Wonderful! We aren't lacking anything we need to live the life that pleases God. Yet, in the next breath he tells us to make every effort to add godliness to our faith. How are we to understand this? Is our holiness up to God or us? As my seminary theol-ogy professor often said about seeming contradictions in Scripture, "The answer is both/and."

Our holiness is wrought by the Spirit's power working through our obedient cooperation. Our salvation is solely God's work, but our sancti-fication is a joint project, a partnership between each of us and God. We can't do it without God's power, and God chooses to do it through our disciplined effort. God gives the power we need for our efforts to affect the condition of our faith.

We see this truth throughout the New Testament. For instance, in a passage we read last week, Paul emphasized the necessity of a believer's effort in the pursuit of a godly life in his first letter to the young pastor, Timothy.

Week 6
Day 1
132
Read 1 Timothy 4:7–8. (Paul uses the same Greek word for "godliness" we found in 2 Peter.)

The Greek word translated as "training" or "exercise" is *gymnazo*. Does it look familiar? We get the English word gymnasium from this Greek word.

Considering what happens in a gym, what do you think Paul meant when he told Timothy to train himself to be godly?

Any athlete who wants to do well in his or her sport must commit to regular physical training. This commitment requires discipline, dedication, and a plan, like Missy Franklin's diligent training schedule. Paul used the example of an athlete to illustrate a spiritual truth. Holiness won't happen by acci-dent or haphazard effort.

A believer's pursuit of holiness must include a commitment to spiritual disciplines. In his book, *Spiritual Disciplines for the Christian Life*, Donald Whit-ney emphasizes their importance. "The only road to Christian maturity and godliness passes through the practice of the Spiritual Disciplines. . . . Godliness is the goal of the Disciplines." Whitney defines *spiritual disciplines* as "those personal and corporate disciplines that promote spiritual growth. . . . They are the God-given means we are to use in the Spirit-filled pursuit of godliness."

While you may see slightly different lists or additional disciplines from other scholars and teachers, those Whitney covers in his book is a well-rounded collection:

- Bible intake
- Prayer
- Worship
- Evangelism
- Service
- Stewardship
- Fasting
- Silence and solitude
- Journaling
- Learning

Look back through the list above. Which of these disciplines is a regular part of your life?

How would you describe your commitment to spiritual disciplines?
___ Nonexistent
___ Haphazard
___ Inconsistent
___ Faithful, but limited in scope
___ Strong and vital

An in-depth look at spiritual disciplines is beyond the scope of our study. However, since their practice is vital to our holiness, we needed to touch on them today. If you need to know more about what spiritual disciplines are or how to practice them, Whitney's book is a great starting point. There are also many other great resources available.

As we end today, give some serious thought to your practice of spiritual disciplines. Wherever you are in your commitment to this effort to seek holiness, I encourage you to take a new step. For instance, I've been faithful to Bible study and prayer for a long time, but in recent years God impressed me with the need to "hide His Word in my heart." So, I began to systematically memorize Scripture.

Spend a few moments asking God about your commitment to spiritual disciplines. Is there something you need to add? Do you need to make a commitment for the first time? Write what God shows you below.

dead or alive

I'm going to use an ugly word. It even has four letters. In fact, my editor may simply black it out. But it case it gets through, get ready. Are you ready? Here it comes.

Obey.

Did you cringe? Yesterday we discussed the importance of spiritual disciplines in our pursuit of holiness. Today, we're going to tackle a tough topic that is absolutely vital to our holiness—obedience. Without obedience we cannot live the holy life that pleases God. Unfortunately, many preachers and teachers avoid talking about obedience these days. Some are afraid they will run people off. Granted, our sin nature doesn't like to be told what to do, but unless we talk about obedience we're falling far short of Jesus' call to make disciples.

Turning away from sin and yielding our will to God's will leads to holiness. But obedience can be hard. And the world constantly bombards us with contradictory "wisdom."

Do you sometimes find it hard to obey God? List everything you can think of that makes obedience difficult.

Many times, sin appears fun and exciting. And the world tells us that we shouldn't have to answer to anyone. That obedience to God is just too hard. That as long as we aren't hurting anyone we can do what we want, what feels good. There's just one problem with that. Disobedience to God always hurts. There are always consequences.

So many times we want to obey, but it seems sin just gets the best of us. This does not have to be! In Week 4, we explored the glorious truth that through His death and resurrection Jesus defeated death and broke the hold of sin. In fact, take a moment now and quickly review Week 4, Day 4.

What direct commands to believers did you find in Romans 6:11–14?

Based on these commands, would you say God wants you to obey Him? Circle one of the following.

Yes   No   Only when it's easy   When I want to   I have no idea

Believers, God calls us to obedience, but He does not leave us floundering on our own. Jesus' work in salvation is also our spiritual reality. We are no longer slaves to sin. It has no power over us. In fact, we are filled with the mighty *dunamis* power of God's Spirit. It's a double-whammy. Sin has no power over us and we have divine power to obey God. Sounds great, but how do we live this out day to day?

Read Romans 8:5–8. According to Paul, what are the two possible directions for our lives?

What is the outcome for each possibility?

Read Romans 8:9–14.

Paul begins this section by reminding his readers that as believers they do not have to follow after their fleshly desires because they are no longer slaves to sin. The same is true for you. If you are a Christian, your life has been redeemed from slavery to sin. You are dead to sin and alive to Christ. You are His bondservant with His Spirit living in you. You have been set free from sin with the power to say no to temptation and yes to God.

🗝 Look back at Romans 8:11–14. Because God has saved us and given us His Spirit, what "obligation" do we have as believers? (Mark all that apply.)

___ To follow our sinful nature and submit to its desires

___ To turn away from the deeds of our sinful nature

___ To submit to the leading of the Holy Spirit

Believers are obligated to say no to sin and instead yield to the leadership of the Holy Spirit. Believers never have to say yes to sin. The devil cannot make us do anything. Temptation will never be so strong that we cannot resist.

🗝 Read 1 Corinthians 10:13. Rewrite God's promise in your own words.

God is faithful. When we are tempted, He will always give us an escape route. Unfortunately, sometimes we don't look for it. I challenge us to do this: the next time we're tempted, let's send up a prayer and ask God to show us the "way out" He has provided. Then let's take it!

Our second obligation we see in the Romans passage is to follow the leading of the Holy Spirit. A lifestyle of obedience is not harsh legalism — stringently abiding by a set of rules. Instead, obedience is following the moment-by-moment leadership of the Holy Spirit. And as we listen and obey, God will be transforming us into a reflection of His holiness.

In his letter to the Christians in Galatia, Paul elaborates on the outcome of our choice to either follow our sinful nature or the Holy Spirit. We also read this passage last week, but let's take another look.

Read Galatians 5:16–25. Are we told to produce the fruit of the Spirit? (Circle one.)

Yes   No

🗝 Identify two things found in Galatians 5:16–25 that believers should be doing.

1.

2.

By definition, *fruit* is the natural by-product of the Holy Spirit. As we "crucify" our sinful nature and live by the Spirit, our old passions and desires will begin to die and the character of Christ will be manifest in us. The rotten fruit will fall away and the fruit of God's holiness will grow in its place.

Verse 24 clearly shows the believer is responsible for crucifying her sinful nature. When we consider other Scriptures, we learn this must be a daily, ongoing discipline. For instance, in Luke 9:23, Jesus emphasized the daily need to deny our sinful nature and follow Him instead. "Then he said to them all: 'Whoever wants to be my disciple must deny themselves and take up their cross daily and follow me.'" We cannot grow the fruit of the Spirit and we cannot transform our character, but we can turn away from our sinful desires and follow the Holy Spirit—today, tomorrow, and for the rest of our lives.

Reread Galatians 5:25 in the three different translations below.

> *Since we are living by the Spirit, let us follow the Spirit's leading in every part of our lives.* (NLT)

> *If we live by the [Holy] Spirit, let us also walk by the Spirit. [If by the Holy Spirit we have our life in God, let us go forward walking in line, our conduct controlled by the Spirit.]* (AMP)

> *Since we live by the Spirit, let us keep in step with the Spirit.* (NIV)

In each translation, go back and circle Paul's specific directive to believers about what we should do since we live by the Spirit.

The Greek word that is translated in this variety of ways is *stoicheō*. It signifies to walk in a line or a row, in relation to someone else or to keep in step with another person, like soldiers marching together in formation. For believers, that means we are to watch the Holy Spirit's steps and follow closely. We are to emulate His every move.

Considering the definition of *stoicheō*, what would it look like in your daily life to keep in step with, walk by, and follow the Holy Spirit?

This truth reminds me of the childhood game "follow the leader." The group selects a leader and everyone lines up behind him. The object of the game is to see how closely you can mimic the leader's movements. If the leader runs ahead 20 steps and then turns to the right, you run ahead 20 steps and then turn to the right. If the leader jumps in the air and spins around three times, you jump in the air and spin around three times. (Of course, that's when I'd fall over from dizziness and be thrown out of the game.)

Playing "follow the leader" is much easier than following the Holy Spirit. Even though the power of sin has been broken and we have the Holy Spirit empowering us from within, we are still prone to weakness and temptations. We will still fall, but we must get up and keep going. Holiness is a process. Charles Stanley writes about this in his book, *Living in the Power of the Holy Spirit*.

> "Life in the Spirit becomes our desire, but that life is not automatically acquired. We must learn to walk in that new life, learn to think in a new way that the Bible calls the 'renewal of the mind,' and develop new ways of responding to life's problems and circumstances."

The Holy Spirit is our teacher and we are the student. He is our leader and we are the follower. We must line up behind Him and watch His every move. We do as He directs. One thing Stanley mentioned that will help us recognize His leading and obey Him is to bring our thinking in line with His. In tomorrow's lesson, we will explore what it means to renew our minds so our thinking will reflect God's truth.

As we close today, ask God to sensitize you to the leadership of the Holy Spirit. Ask Him to give you a desire to say no to sin, yield your own will to His, and obey.

a new attitude

If "you are what you eat" is true, then I'm a handful of chocolate-covered coffee beans sprinkled on top of a huge bowl of ice cream. Yes, I consume a lot of chocolate, coffee, and ice cream. And while I also eat lean meat and fresh fruits and veggies, I'm sure I would be healthier if I cut back on my favorites.

Everyone recognizes our diets directly affect the health and working of our bodies. And while we may not eat right 100 percent of the time, many of us try to do what's best for our bodies overall.

But are we as careful with our spiritual health? The Bible shows a direct correlation between what we put into our minds and our outward actions. The way we think directly affects our character, behavior, and holiness. Last week, I told you about a fiction book series I had been reading and the effect it had on my thinking. Thankfully, the words that popped into my head didn't come out of my mouth, but I don't doubt they would have had I continued to read the books. God quickly and clearly showed me the connection between what I allowed into my mind and my behavior.

Yesterday, we learned we will either live our lives following after our "sinful nature" or the Holy Spirit. In Romans 8, which we studied yesterday, Paul directly links the way we think to what we will follow (i.e., obey). Douglas Moo elaborates in his commentary on Romans.

> In verses 5–8, then, Paul presents a series of contrasts between flesh and Spirit. His overall intention is clear: to show that *sarx* (flesh) brings death while the Spirit brings life (v. 6). Paul leads up to this key claim by tracing people's manner of life to their underlying way of thinking. . . . The lifestyle of the flesh flows from a mind oriented to the flesh, whereas the lifestyle of the Spirit comes from a mind oriented to the Spirit."

✏️ In the space below, write every reason you can think of for why our thinking impacts our behavior.

Let's revisit a passage we read in our first day of study last week. In his letter to the Christians in Rome, Paul also emphasized the connection between our thinking and our spiritual condition.

🗝️ Read Romans 12:1–2. Christ's sacrifice for our salvation demands a response. What is it? (Mark all that apply.)
____ Give your whole self to God as a holy, living sacrifice.
____ Reject and turn away from the behavior and thinking of the world.
____ Allow God to transform you into the image of His Son.
____ Live a life that pleases God by obeying Him.

Verse 2 contains a phrase we can't ignore if we want to respond to God in these ways. Paul says our spiritual transformation occurs through the renewing of our minds. According to *Vine's Complete Expository Dictionary*, the noun *renewing* means "the adjustment of the moral and spiritual vision and thinking to the mind of God, which is designed to have a transforming effect upon the life."

The way we think will dictate our behavior. For instance, if we repeatedly and exclusively hear society's view that God's teaching on sexual relationships is outdated and waiting for marriage is ridiculous, then we are likely to have sex outside of marriage. But if we learn about God's perfect design for sexuality and marriage and accept His Word as timeless truth, it's more likely our behavior will line up with that thinking.

What our culture considers "good, moral, and acceptable" is a far cry from the truth of God's Word. When we watch, read, and participate in things out of line with God's truth our thinking becomes desensitized. As our thinking shifts and conforms to the world our character and behavior will follow. We will do what we think.

The Holy Spirit is the agent of renewal (Titus 3:5), but we can cooperate with His work by feeding our mind with truth. Let's ask God to show us where our thinking is out of line with His truth. Let's ask Him to renew our thinking and transform our spiritual health. And we can cooperate with Him in practical ways. Let's start right now.

Read Philippians 4:8. What are God's guidelines for how we should invest our thinking time?

Honestly evaluate what you're feeding your own mind. Fill out the table below to get an overall picture. I've filled in a few blanks to get you started. Be as honest and as comprehensive as possible. Continue on a separate sheet of paper if needed.

Source of Brain "Food"	Amount of Time Spent Per Week	Percent That Meets Philippians 4:8 Standards	How This Source Shapes Your Thinking
television/ movies			
music			
social media/ internet			
Bible reading			
books			

Did anything surprise you as you completed the table? Maybe the amount of time you spend each week feeding your mind with things that don't reflect God's truth shocked you. Maybe you thought you spend more time filling your mind with the truth of God's Word than you actually do.

🌱 What things on your list above do you feel have the most negative impact on your thinking? Ask God if He wants you to reduce or eliminate any of these. Record what He tells you below.

🌱 We need to purposefully work to break down a secular worldview and build a biblical worldview. List every way you can think of that we can feed our minds with the truth of God's Word and override the lies from our culture. (Keep in mind, not every message from our culture is false. Knowing God's truth will help us discern truth from lie.)

Our spiritual transformation and the renewing of our minds is an ongoing process. We must continue to reject the leanings of our old sinful nature. We must continually override the "wisdom" of the world by allowing God's truth to reprogram our thinking. Old patterns and habits are not easy to break. It takes time and relentless vigilance.

The more we renew our thinking, the more clearly we will discern the guidance of the Holy Spirit. Since our thinking will be lining up with His, there will be less confusion and more clarity. Our minds will be set on what the Spirit desires and our lives will be holy and pleasing to God.

As we close, commit to God at least one thing you will do today to start moving your thinking in line with His.

practicality, part 1

We've come a long way in our journey toward holiness. So, how are you doing? Do you have a better understanding of holiness, God's call, and our need to pursue it?

My prayer for you today is twofold. First, that God will fill you with a desire to be holy. And second, as you diligently desire holiness you'll find yourself wrapped in the loving embrace of our holy God. I want that for you and me!

With just two days remaining to spend together, it's time to get really practical. We've learned a lot, but I want to help equip us to live out God's truth in our every day lives. Today and tomorrow we will cover six concrete things we can incorporate into our lives to foster holiness. So put on your work gloves and let's dig in!

1. PRACTICE AN AWARENESS OF THE PRESENCE OF GOD

Scripture teaches and Christians accept with faith that God is omnipresent. All of Him is present everywhere, all the time. But so often, since we live in a physical world that we experience with our five senses, we fail to live in actuality what we accept intellectually. We believe God is present with us, but we rarely experience His presence. A. W. Tozer elaborates on this in *The Pursuit of God*.

> Our trouble is that we have established bad thought habits. We habitually think of the visible world as real and doubt the reality of the other. We do not deny the existence of the spiritual world but we doubt that it is real in the accepted meaning of the word. . . . Sin has so clouded the lenses of our hearts that we cannot see that other reality, the City of God, shining around us. The world of sense triumphs. The visible becomes the enemy of the invisible, the temporal, of the eternal.

I can certainly identify with what Tozer wrote. I often struggle to keep a grip on the imminent reality of the spiritual. I allow the concrete presence of the physical world to crowd the presence of God from my mind. However, it seems King David had a better grasp on the reality of God's presence.

Read Psalm 139:1–12. What implications does God's omnipresence and omniscience (all knowledge) have? List everything you can find.

God is always with us. He sees everything we do. He knows our thoughts, attitudes, and motivations. How could purposefully remembering this impact our pursuit of holiness?

Maintaining an awareness of God's presence gladdens our heart, nourishes our soul, and feeds our holiness. To foster an awareness of His presence, we must be disciplined and intentional. Here are a few, quick suggestions:

- Regularly reflect on His holy character.

- Determine a means to remind yourself to concentrate on Him throughout the day. (For instance, maybe at the top of every hour.)

- Allow your thoughts to momentarily rest on Him at multiple times during the day.

- Form a habit of talking to Him throughout the day, even about mundane things.

List below every way you can think of that will help you foster a constant awareness of God's presence. Think outside the box!

2. STAY IN THE WORD

The Bible is a miracle. It was written over a period of 1,500 years, penned by more than 40 different authors in three different languages. Although, no original manuscripts remain, overwhelming evidence exists to support the Christian belief that what we have today is what God originally gave to us. The Creator of the universe revealed Himself to man and then wonderfully preserved it for Christians throughout history. God's Word to us.

I fell in love with God's Word during my first women's Bible study when I was a young mom. Although I entered into a saving relationship with Jesus when I was eight, my spiritual growth was negligible until I began spending regular time reading and studying the Bible. I had missed so much by neglecting His Word! Through the Bible, God reveals His nature and His ways. He shows us how to live holy lives that please Him and strengthens our relationships with Him. We will be spiritually hindered without ongoing interaction with God's Word.

The Bible itself testifies to the importance of God's Word in our lives. Read Psalm 119:1–16. Based on this passage, mark the following statements true or false. (Watch for synonyms used for the Bible such as *word, laws, statutes, precepts, decrees,* and *commands.*)

Week 6
Day 4
145

_____ Those who want to be holy will live according to God's Word.

_____ Those who seek God and long to find Him will obey His Word.

_____ God expects us to know and obey His Word.

_____ We will find joy and delight in obeying God's Word.

We cannot live by God's Word unless we know God's Word. List below all the ways you can think of to learn and know the Bible. Beside each way, note how much time you spend a week in this activity.

How does the amount of time you spend taking in God's Word compare to the amount of time you spend on other brain food activities? (Refer back to the table you completed yesterday about your sources of brain food.)

3. MAKE THE MOST OF TRIALS

Stress makes our muscles bigger and stronger. When we lift a heavier load than our muscles have lifted before, a physical process begins to adapt the needed muscles to the new load. Without stress, our muscles are content with their current size and strength. Add stress, and our muscles begin to change to meet the need.

Our spiritual muscles are similar. The difficulties of life stress our faith. Trials work our faith the way heavy loads work our muscles. As we faithfully endure, we grow spiritually stronger. Without difficulty, our faith tends to stagnate.

While we must go out of our way to lift weights to build physical strength, there's no need for us to seek out trials to build our spiritual strength. They are sure to come! Jesus Himself said, "In this world you will have trouble. But take heart! I have overcome the world" (John 16:33). Our goal in the midst of these trials is to lean on Jesus and trust Him to be faithful. As we receive His strength and follow His leading, we will grow spiritually and become more like Him. While trails can be painful and cumbersome, God promises to use them for our good. Let's take a closer look at what God can do.

Read James 1:2–4 and 1 Peter 1:6–7. In your own words, describe how God uses trials and difficulties in our lives.

What things can believers do in the midst of trials to ensure we get the most out of God's refining fire?

Today, we've talked about three practical things we can do to foster holiness in our lives. We will consider three more tomorrow. As we close today, I encourage you to reflect on these first three.

Spend a few moments in prayer. Ask God to show you if you need to make any attitude adjustments or behavior changes based on what you've learned today. Record what He tells you.

practicality, part 2

This is our last day together. I so wish we could sit down, have a cup of coffee together, and chat for a while. I'd love to hear about what God has been doing in your life through this study. I'd even bring chocolate to share! Oh, maybe one day. But today I'll have to settle for sharing three more practical ways we can foster holiness in our lives. Let's continue yesterday's topic.

4. RESPOND QUICKLY TO THE HOLY SPIRIT

Did you know the Holy Spirit has a job description? He has distinctive work to carry out in the life of every believer. For instance, He brought new life to your sin dead spirit and He equipped you with gifts to use in service and ministry. And in this study, we've learned how the Spirit transforms and empowers us.

At the risk of repeating myself, I want to zero in on one task in particular. We've covered it at length, but it's too important to leave out of our six practical ways to foster holiness.

Read Romans 8:13–14. Based on this passage, what task would you add to the Spirit's job description?

Now read Galatians 5:25. How are we to respond to this work of the Holy Spirit?

On a general level, the Holy Spirit's leading includes guiding us away from sin and into holiness. He helps us resist temptation and obey God's moral commands. But His leading is also very personal. In *Systematic Theology: An Introduction to Biblical Doctrine*, Wayne Grudem writes that the leading of the Holy Spirit Paul talks about in Galatians 5 "implies an active personal participation by the Holy Spirit in guiding us. This is something more than our reflecting on biblical moral standards, and includes an involvement by the Holy Spirit in relating to us as persons and leading and directing us."

The following verses record instances when the Spirit guided believers very personally in specific situations. Read each passage and record the type of direction the Spirit gave.

Acts 8:29

Acts 13:2

Acts 15:27–29

Acts 16:6–7

Acts 20:22–23

The Holy Spirit convicts believers of sin, points us to righteousness, encourages us to good works, counsels us in decisions, informs us in dilemmas, and guides us into God's will for us.

Considering the work of the Holy Spirit in our lives, how important is it that we obey Him? How can we foster quick and complete obedience?

If we hesitate or fail to obey, what could be some of the consequences?

5. BE PROACTIVE IN YOUR BATTLE AGAINST SIN

I hate weeds. They are a pervasive problem, and we have a large yard. Unfortunately, I seem to be the only one in my family who cares about this unsightly blight, so I fight the battle alone.

Since I have lots of experience in the war against weeds, allow me to share a few tips. First, when pulling existing weeds, make sure you get all of the root, or they'll come right back. For large, tough weeds, use a spade to loosen the soil and dig deep. Show no mercy! Second, prevention saves a lot of time and spares much pain. Use weed barrier in beds and preemergent treatment on the lawn. The best kind of weed is one that never grows in the first place.

I know you know where I'm going with this. Weeds in the yard are like sin in our lives. We must root out existing sin and get rid of it. And we must recognize areas of weakness to guard against potential sin.

Read James 4:1–4. How did James's Christian audience get caught in this cycle of sin?

Now read James 4:6–10. List all the words and phrases that describe the actions a Christian should take when she's chosen to follow her own sinful nature instead of the Spirit.

Believers, these actions characterize true repentance. Sometimes we Christians merely give lip service to repentance. We must humble ourselves before God, grieve over our sin, and turn away from it. And when we do, our faithful and just God will "forgive us our sins and purify us from all unrighteousness" (1 John 1:9).

Real repentance can be a painful process. Although we won't be able to rid our lives of sin completely, we can reduce the amount we fall by following the advice Jesus gave His disciples in the garden on the night He was arrested.

Read Mark 14:38. What two things did Jesus tell them to do to avoid following into sin?

The Greek word translated as "watch" in the NIV means "a mindfulness of threatening dangers, which, with conscious earnestness and an alert mind, keeps one from all drowsiness and all slackening in the energy of faith and conduct." When Jesus told the disciples to "watch and pray," He wanted them to recognize potential sin danger and guard themselves against falling. How did they do?

🌱 Prayerfully consider where the areas of weakness are in your life. Maybe it's overeating or speech or greed or sex. Ask the Holy Spirit to show you specific ways you can protect yourself from falling in this area. Record what He shows you below.

Until our physical lives are over, we will continue to sin. But praise God, He freely forgives us when we repent! However, let's also cultivate holiness by guarding ourselves against sin. "Be alert and of sober mind. Your enemy the devil prowls around like a roaring lion looking for someone to devour" (1 Peter 5:8). Sisters, let's watch and pray and draw close to the Holy One!

6. KEEP AN ETERNAL PERSPECTIVE
The need to live with an eternal perspective is a truth principle God has been patiently planting in my heart and soul for a while. I must be a slow learner because He keeps bringing it up. If we don't stay focused on God's bigger, eternal picture, then the things of this physical world and the status of our temporal circumstances will drive our emotions and responses.

Describe what you think it means to live with an eternal perspective instead of a temporal one.

🗝 God's children described in the Hebrews Hall of Faith most certainly lived with an eternal perspective. Read Hebrews 11:13–16. What do you see in this passage that shows they lived with an eternal perspective?

🌱 Describe how keeping an eternal perspective would affect the way you would react or respond in the following situations:

You've been diagnosed with a chronic or terminal illness.

Your neighbors do not know Jesus.

You have a great opportunity to move up in your company, but it means compromising God's standards.

Your marriage is in bad shape, and a co-worker of the opposite sex has been extremely comforting.

The author of Hebrews writes that Moses "chose to be mistreated along with the people of God rather than to enjoy the fleeting pleasures of sin" (Hebrews 11:25). He rejected sin and persevered through hard times because he saw "him who is invisible" (v. 27). Moses' eternal perspective fostered holiness in his life, which paved the way for a deep intimacy with God. "The LORD would speak to Moses face to face, as one speaks to a friend" (Exodus 33:11).

Believers, just imagine the joy! Daily living in close intimacy with the One who made you. No division, no distance. Face-to-face and heart-to-heart.

Into His Arms! Embracing a Life of Holiness

Stacy loves Jesus and purposefully seeks to follow Him closely. For instance, each morning, she takes time to focus on the gospel of Christ. "When I saw the movie *The Passion of the Christ* for the first time, I left the theater thinking, *I don't ever want to sin again!* But of course, I have. But remembering what Jesus did to make me His, keeps me centered on God and fosters my desire to be holy."

Another thing that keeps Stacy committed to holiness is remembering that God is always with her. "As a believer, I am God's temple. His Spirit lives in me. He is always with me and He is always watching. I constantly ask myself: 'If God were here physically in the room, would it change the way I act or what I watch or what I say?'"

Stacy also submits herself to accountability. She shares sin struggles and areas of weaknesses with a trusted friend and gives them permission to hold her accountable. "One time, just the confession of a sin to another person helped me see it for what it was. That alone gave me deliverance. And knowing someone is likely to ask me about a specific area can keep me standing firm."

Even with her practical and intentional discipleship, Stacy still sometimes falls. Not long ago, Stacy and her husband invited another couple over for dinner. At one point in the evening, the conversation turned to a woman who had hurt Stacy years earlier. Stacy went through the entire situation with her dinner guests. She dredged up all the details and laid it out for everyone to see how she'd been wronged.

The next morning, Stacy woke with conviction heavy on her heart. She thought she had forgiven the woman, but bitterness and unforgiveness had risen to the surface. And she had gossiped about the woman with her husband and two close friends. Stacy's sin had impacted other people and strained her relationship with God.

Following the leading of the Spirit, she confessed her sin to God. Then she asked her husband and friends for their forgiveness. While this experience was embarrassing and humbling it encouraged her to cling even tighter to holiness. Stacy didn't want anything to cause distance between her and God.

Make a list of the intentional things Stacy does to pursue Christ and grow in holiness.

What other spiritual disciplines, attitudes, or activities can you think of that would foster holiness and deepen your relationship with God?

Which of these are included in your life now? What do you think God would have you incorporate in your intentional pursuit of holiness?

How did Stacy respond when God convicted her of sin? What do you think would have happened if she had ignored the Spirit's prompting?

How do you usually respond to the Holy Spirit's conviction? Prayerfully ask God if there is an unresolved sin issue in your life now that you need to deal with.

My heart is full as I write these last words to you—my fellow sojourner on the path to holiness. God has taught me, challenged me, and drawn me close during my time of study. I'm praying He has done the same for you these past six weeks. As you continue to grow in holiness, may our holy God wrap you in His loving embrace.

leader guide

Thank you for your willingness to serve God by leading a small group through this study of His Word. Together, we will spend the next six weeks discovering how holiness fosters an intimate, growing relationship with God. It will be exciting to watch the women in your group draw closer to God as they begin to strive for holiness.

Feel free to use the suggestions in this guide or adapt them as God leads. You know the needs of the women in your group. Ask God to apply the biblical truths found in the study to your life and the lives of the women in your group. Ask Him to help you lead the group in a way that fosters what He wants to do in their lives.

Here are a few things you'll need to know as you work through the study:

- I used an NIV Bible to prepare fill-in-the-blank and matching questions.

- The "key" icon is used to mark questions that deal with key truths from that day of study.

- The "grow" icon is used to mark "Grow" questions; "Grow" questions are designed to help students personally apply the biblical truths.

- Some of the "Grow" questions are very personal. When asking them in the group, feel free to make them more general to avoid any embarrassment and to encourage discussion.

May God bless you and your group as you strive to live holy lives!

Kathy

introductory week

Many Bible study groups meet the first week to hand out books, get to know one another, and simply kick things off. You may also be given the opportunity for your small group to meet, but of course your group members won't have any completed study material to discuss until the following week.

Don't panic! If you have some time together that first week, make the most of it. Here are a few suggestions:

1. ICEBREAKER—Search the Internet for a fun activity that will help the women get to know each other better. This is a great way to create a comfortable atmosphere for your group.

2. DISCUSSION—Introduce our study topic with a brief discussion that will generate interest for the week ahead. You can prepare by getting your book in advance and completing the first week of study ahead of your group. Here are a few questions to try:

   (Leader Guide 155

   Would you use the word holy to describe yourself? Why or why not?

   Do you think God wants you to be holy? Why or why not?

   What does it mean to for a Christian to be holy? What does it look like in daily life?

3. PRAYER—Pray together as a group. Do it however you think the ladies will be the most comfortable. For instance, you can take verbal requests and you lead in prayer, break up into groups of two or three, or do "popcorn" prayer around the room.

every study week

The following suggestions apply to all six weeks of study. (See below for suggestions specific to the individual weeks.) Arrange them and adapt them to meet the specific needs of your group.

1. PRAYER—There is potential for great spiritual growth during this study. The enemy does not want you and your women to grow. Please be

diligent to cover your group and your study in prayer. I also encourage your group to pray together each week. You can do this at the beginning or the end of your time. You can do it in various ways — prayer partners, entire group, popcorn prayer, email requests, etc. — just pray!

2. INTRODUCE THE WEEK'S PRIMARY TRUTHS — Open the discussion each week with a quick overview of the primary truths. (These truths are listed below for each week.) Then ask the group what impacted them the most during the week.

3. STUDY QUESTIONS — Use the "Key" 🗝 and "Grow" 🌱 questions from each day of study to guide discussion in your group. The combination of these two types of questions will encourage learning and spiritual growth.

4. ADDITIONAL QUESTIONS — Enhance your discussion using any or all of the additional questions I've provided below for each week. Feel free to toss in your own questions too!

5. INTO HIS ARMS — Each week of study concludes with a story about a real person dealing with real faith issues. The story and the following questions will help you and your group to understand how that week's biblical principles can apply to your daily lives. Read the story out loud to the group, then use the questions to kick-start discussion about how to apply that week's biblical truths.

week one
PRIMARY TRUTHS
- God is transcendent in His holiness.
- God's call to us to live holy lives.
- Our holiness matters to God.
ADDITIONAL QUESTIONS
- Why should we be holy?
- What scares or concerns you about trying to live a holy life?
- How is a life of holiness also a life of freedom?

week two
PRIMARY TRUTHS
- God wants us to know Him and invites us to experience Him.
- God reveals His holy nature to us through nature, the Bible, and His Son.
- God's people should prepare themselves to encounter His holiness.

ADDITIONAL QUESTIONS
- Share about a time that God's creation moved you to praise and worship Him.
- In what ways have you taken Jesus too "casually"?
- How do you think experiencing God's holiness like Moses did would affect you?
- Summarize how believers can prepare to experience God's holiness.

week three
PRIMARY TRUTHS
- Intellectual assent to God's holiness is not the same as experiencing it.
- God's holiness demands an appropriate response.

ADDITIONAL QUESTIONS
- What are some of the ways people respond to God's holiness today?
- What is the appropriate response to God's holiness?
- How should the truth that God is holy affect the way we respond to life's trials?

week four
PRIMARY TRUTHS
- We are positionally holy before God through the Cross of Christ.
- Christ takes our sin and gives us His righteousness.
- God has given us everything we need to live a holy life.

ADDITIONAL QUESTIONS
- Explain what it means to be "positionally" holy before God.
- How can we be both "holy" and "becoming holy?"
- In what ways are Jesus' death, burial, and resurrection a spiritual reality in the lives of believers?

week five
PRIMARY TRUTHS
- God calls His children to ever-increasing holiness.
- God's standard for holiness never changes.
- Holiness brings blessings.

ADDITIONAL QUESTIONS
- Define progressive holiness.
- Do you measure your holiness by the world's standards or God's?
- How does sin hinder our relationship with God?
- How does a holy life draw us closer to God?

PRIMARY TRUTHS

- Our holiness is a cooperative effort between each of us and God.
- Our personal holiness requires diligent effort.
- The Holy Spirit supplies the power for holiness when we obediently follow Him.
- The way we think will drive our behavior.
- Believers can practically and purposefully work toward holiness.

ADDITIONAL QUESTIONS

- Describe the partnership that should exist between a believer and the Holy Spirit.
- How do spiritual disciplines help us in our pursuit of holiness?
- How is following the Spirit different from legalistically following a set of rules?
- What can believers do to line up our thinking with God's?
- Name the six concrete things we can do to purposefully pursue holiness.

New Hope® Publishers is a division of WMU®, an international orga-
nization that challenges Christian believers to understand and be radically
involved in God's mission. For more information about WMU,
go to wmu.com. More information about New Hope books may be
found at NewHopeDigital.com. New Hope books may be
purchased at your local bookstore.

Use the QR reader on your
smartphone to visit us online at
NewHopeDigital.com

If you've been blessed by this book, we would like to hear your story.
The publisher and author welcome your comments and
suggestions at: newhopereader@wmu.org.

Engage.

Equip.

Encourage.

New Hope Publishers Women in Bible Study online community offers a place for women to engage with our best-selling Bible study authors, share experiences and insight, and learn of resources, both in print and online, that will help both Bible study leaders and participants grow deeper in their walk with Christ.

From relevant topics such as prayer, relationships, growth, lifestyle, and mentoring, there is something for women. Whether you've been engaged in Bible study your whole life or just getting started, the New Hope Women in Bible Study community will engage, equip, and encourage every woman seeking to live a godly life.

To learn more visit **NewHopeDigital.com/women.**

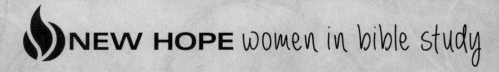